Index

Deal 1

This book in my Bridge Lesson Series really gets to the nitty-gritty of the game: how to assess the worth of your hand in the bidding, so you contract for an appropriate number of tricks in the play.

We will of course be using the familiar High Card Point Count (ace = 4, king = 3, queen = 2, jack = 1); but looking much deeper. We will be lauding the Losing Trick Count (LTC) - that method of hand evaluation in fit situations; but also recognising its limitations. Our mission - your ultimate goal - is not to be a slave to points, or to the LTC. To develop judgement.

Exercise: As a taster, what do you think of these 13-point balanced hands? Rate them on a scale of 0 to 10. Having opened 1NT, would you accept an invitational raise to 2NT from partner?

(a)	(b)	(c)	(d)
♠ J 6 2	♠ Q J 3	♠ K 7 2	♠ K J 3
♡ K Q	♡ 9 2	♡ K J 4	♡ Q 10 9 6
◇ Q 8 4 2	◇ K J 10 9 4	◇ K J 6	◇ K 10 9 5
♣ A J 5 2	♣ A Q 6	♣ Q 8 4 2	♣ A 9

(a) 2/10. No tens or nines, too many high cards in the short hearts.

(b) 8/10. Powerful five-card diamond suit including an internal sequence (the ◇109 are lovely) - imagine them facing the queen. Your hearts are poor, but you can't have everything and it's much better to have a trick-source than...

(c) ...the jam too thinly spread. Yuk - where are the tricks coming from here? Poor shape, no sequential honours or intermediates. 1/10 (even that's generous).

(d) 7/10. Nice robust four-card suits - those nines could make all the difference.

(a) and (c) should pass 2NT; (b) and (d) should bid 3NT. In truth, four pretty clear-cut choices. How did you fare?

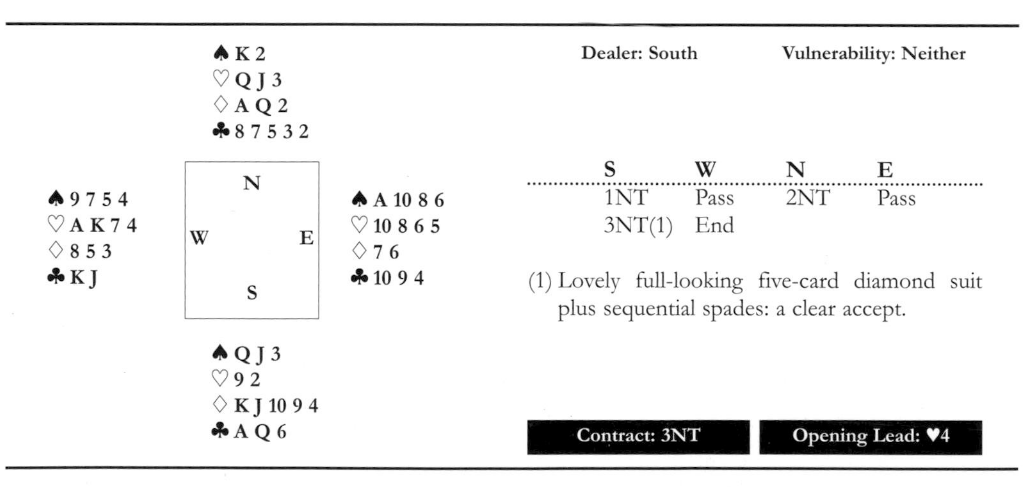

On our deal, South accepted the invite and received the four of hearts lead, dummy's jack winning. Counting seven tricks, he was not tempted to take the club finesse (low to the queen). It would only give him one extra trick, whereas the spade sequence would provide two. Plus he was not overly fearful of hearts: West's (presumably) fourth-highest ♡4 was his lowest so the suit was splitting 4-4.

Declarer led the king of spades at Trick Two. East won the ace, the defence cashed three hearts, but declarer claimed the rest - five diamonds, ♠QJ and ♣A. Game made.

Deal 2

I have always marvelled at the simplicity of the basic Point-Count method for evaluating a Bridge hand: Ace = 4, King = 3, Queen = 2; Jack = 1. Based on the McCampbell count of 1915 and popularised by Milton Work in 1923, it is an integral part of every player's armoury.

Say opener is balanced: his bidding strategy is based on his point-count - as follows:

12-14 points: Open 1NT.

15-16 points: Open One of Suit, rebid Notrumps at lowest level.

17-18 points: Open One of Suit, rebid Notrumps with a jump.

19 points: Open One of Suit, rebid 3NT.

20-22 points: Open 2NT.

When responder hears of partner's point-count he can accurately assess whether to bid for game, 25 points being the guideline.

Exercise: **1♢ - 1♠ - 1NT - ?**

(a)	(b)	(c)
♠ A Q 6 2	♠ Q J 7 3	♠ K 8 5 2
♡ K 9 7	♡ 10 9 2	♡ Q 4
♢ 4 2	♢ J 9	♢ J 10 2
♣ J 10 8 2	♣ A 10 8 2	♣ Q J 10 3

(a) 3NT. Opener has 15-16, so there are 25 points. Don't be surprised though if 3NT fails - it does not always make with 25 points, or always fail with 24. And don't be surprised if ♣108 make all the difference. If your clubs were ♣J432 you'd still have bid 3NT, but clearly have less chance. [Consider partner with ♣Q9].

(b) Pass. The partnership cannot hold 25 points. Might 3NT make? Sure - especially given your ♡109, ♢9 and ♣108. But because it probably won't, you'd pass.

(c) 2NT. Invite game - asking partner to bid 3NT with a maximum (for his 15-16).

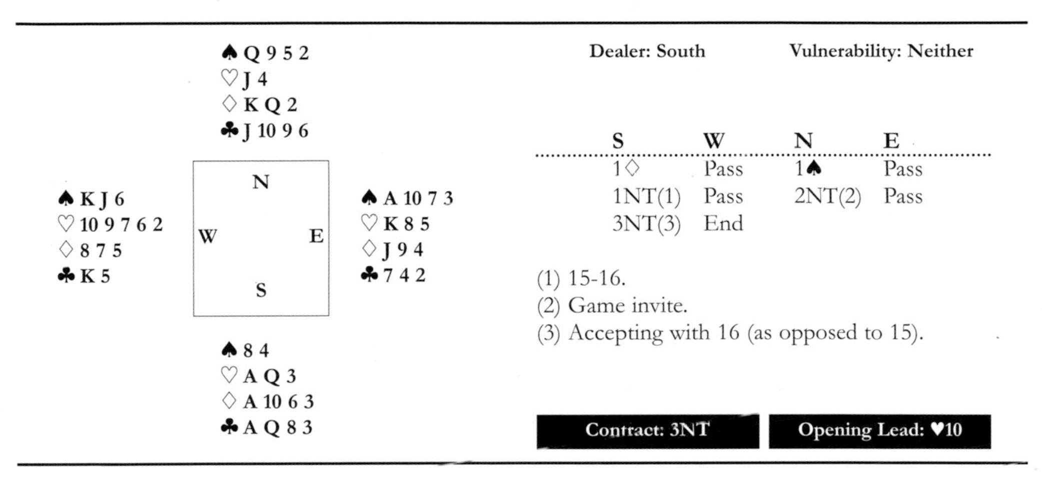

Our deal demonstrates that game does not always make with 25 points. Bad luck (losing the club finesse) and brilliant defence conspired. West led the ten of hearts, to the jack, king and ace. Declarer crossed to the queen of diamonds and ran the jack of clubs to West's king.

Knowing declarer held the queen of hearts (East would have played the queen from ♡KQ), West found the lethal switch to the jack of spades (key play). This went ♠J, ♠Q, ♠A, ♠4. The three was returned to the eight and king, followed by the six through ♠95 to East's ♠107. Down one.

Deal 3

The basic Point-Count system of hand evaluation [Ace = 4, King = 3, Queen = 2; Jack = 1] is nice and easy to learn and apply. In notrumps especially, it is surprisingly effective.

Point-Count is far from perfect however. The Ten gets short-changed; the Ace is worth a bit more than 4; the Jack a bit less than 1. It must be remembered that Point-Count is but a guide. Bridge is all about tricks not points.

Exercise: Partner has opened 1♠ and you have four-card support. The number you bid in support is based on this point-count line:

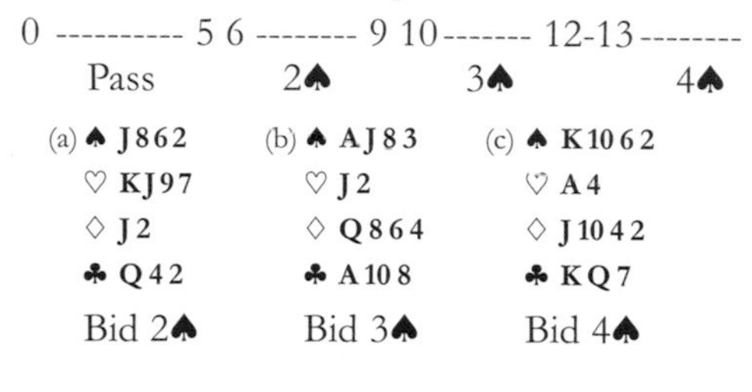

However high-card points are only part of the story. Contrast these three hands in response to a 1♠ opener:

(d)[a]	(e)	(f)
♠ J 8 6 2	♠ J 8 6 4 2	♠ J 8 7 6 4 2
♡ K J 9 7	♡ K J 9 7	♡ K J 9 7
◇ J 2	◇ 2	◇ -
♣ Q 4 2	♣ Q 5 2	♣ Q 5 2

(d) may have one more high-card point than (e) and (f), but is by far the least powerful. The combination of extra trumps and side suit shortage make (e) and - especially - (f) worth much more. Bid 2♠ with (d), 3♠ with (e) and go straight to 4♠ with (f).

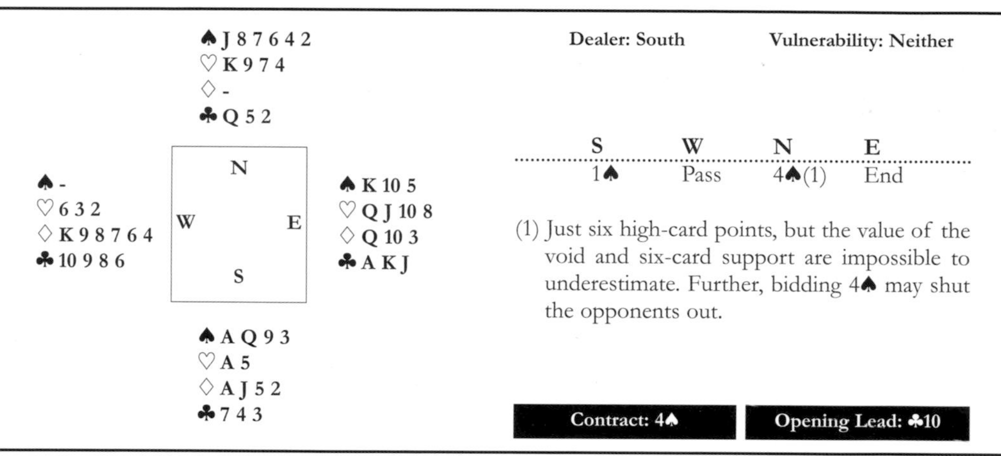

On our deal East won the club lead with the jack and cashed the ace-king, switching to the queen of hearts at Trick Four. Declarer won in dummy to take the trump finesse. Which spade to lead?

Normally you lead a low card, not an honour, when finessing [as you would with ♠Jxxxx facing ♠AQ9x, in case East has a singleton king]. Here, uniquely, missing ♠K10x, you must lead the jack, intending to run it [lead low to the queen and you lose a trick to East's remaining ♠K10 in this layout]. When East covered the jack with the king, declarer won the ace and saw West discard. He was now able to ruff a diamond and lead a second trump to his nine, then cashing the queen felling East's ten. He cashed the red aces and crossruffed for ten tricks - game made.

Deal 4

High card points are pretty accurate for flat hand notrump bidding. 25 points is the guide for 3NT; 33 for 6NT.

Exercise: Respond to partner's (12-14 pt) 1NT opener:

(a)	(b)	(c)	(d)
♠Q 6 2	♠A J 3	♠Q J 3	♠A Q 8
♡J 8 7	♡Q 6 2	♡A K 6	♡A J 9
◇A Q 4 2	◇A 10 7 4	◇A J 10	◇K 9 8 2
♣J 6 2	♣J 9 8	♣A Q 5 2	♣A Q 3

(a) Pass. There cannot be 25 points (partner's maximum is 14).
(b) 2NT. Game invitation.
(c) 6NT. There must be 33 points - no need to faff about.
(d) 4NT. Notrump slam invite (not ace asking following notrumps). As with 2NT, the bid asks partner to bid on with a maximum and pass with a minimum.

High card points only tell part of the story when you have a good fit and some shape (i.e. shortage). Contrast these four hands in suppo of a 1♡ opener:

(e)	(f)	(g)	(h)
♠K 9 7	♠K 9 7	♠K 9 7	♠K 9 7
♡J 7 5 2	♡J 7 5 2	♡J 7 5 2	♡J 7 5 2
◇A J 2	◇A J 7 2	◇A J 8 7 2	◇A J 8 7 3 2
♣9 6 3	♣6 3	♣3	♣-

When you have four-card support for partner (only then), you can add points for shortage: a side-suit doubleton is worth about one extra point; a side-suit singleton three; and a side-suit void five.

Hand (e) has just the nine high card points and would simply raise to 2♡. Hand (f) is worth 10 points - just a 3♡ bid. Hand (g) is worth 12 points and is worth 3½♡ (personally I'd try 4♡- it does pay to be bold with good fits and shape).

Hand (h) contains 9 + 5 = 14 points and is everybody's 4♡ (even a 4♣ splinter bid - if available - showing short clubs in a full game raise).

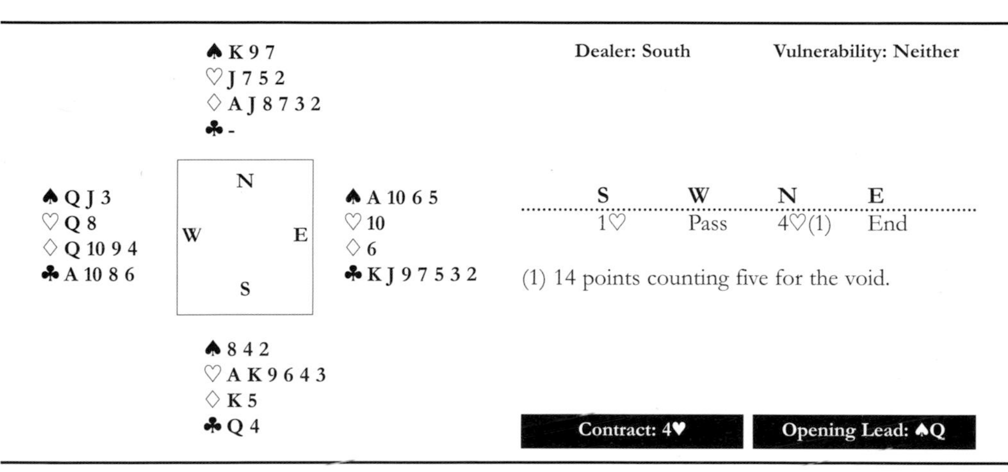

I am not going to dwell on these points for shortage - for two reasons. Firstly because they are at best a rough estimate: facing four small cards, a singleton is fabulous; facing ace-king doubleton, it has no worth. Secondly there is a better method of hand evaluation in these situations... I'm referring to the Losing Trick Count (more next page).

On our deal N-S's 4♡ did not make - due to a devilish defence. West led the queen of spades (winning), the jack of spades (also winning) and a third spade to East's ace. Now the lead of the 13th spade promoted a trick for West's queen of trumps (whether or not declarer ruffed high). E-W were a tad less happy when they realised 5♣ was on...

Deal 5

he basic point-count gives a reasonable valuation of a flattish, notrumpy hand. Hands with trump fits are less simple to evaluate, for side-suit shortages are very valuable. Last page I suggested (when holding four-card support) adding one point for a doubleton, three for a singleton and five for a void. However this really is a 'guesstimate'. Better in such fit situations, short of having years and years of experience, is to use the *Losing Trick Count* (LTC).

First, let's learn how to count up our Losing Tricks. Look at the first three cards of each suit; assume the ace takes the first round, the king the second and the queen the third. How many of those do you not have (up to the number of cards held)? Do this in each suit to obtain total Losing Tricks (LTs).

(a)	(b)	(c)
♠ K 7 2	♠ Q 9 7	♠ A 2
♡ A 9 8 4	♡ K J 6 2	♡ Q 10 8 5 2
◇ 4	◇ A 9 7 3 2	◇ Q 4
♣ 10 9 8 6 2	♣ K	♣ 9 7 6 2

(a) You have two LTs in spades (♠AQ); two in hearts (♡KQ); just one in diamonds (◇A - as you have just one card - you can trump a second round); and three in clubs (♣AKQ - only consider the first three rounds). Total eight LTs.

(b) Two in spades (♠AK), two in hearts (♡AQ), two in diamonds (◇KQ) and one in clubs (♣A fells ♣K). Total seven.

(c) ♠K, ♡AK, ◇AK, ♣AKQ. Total eight.

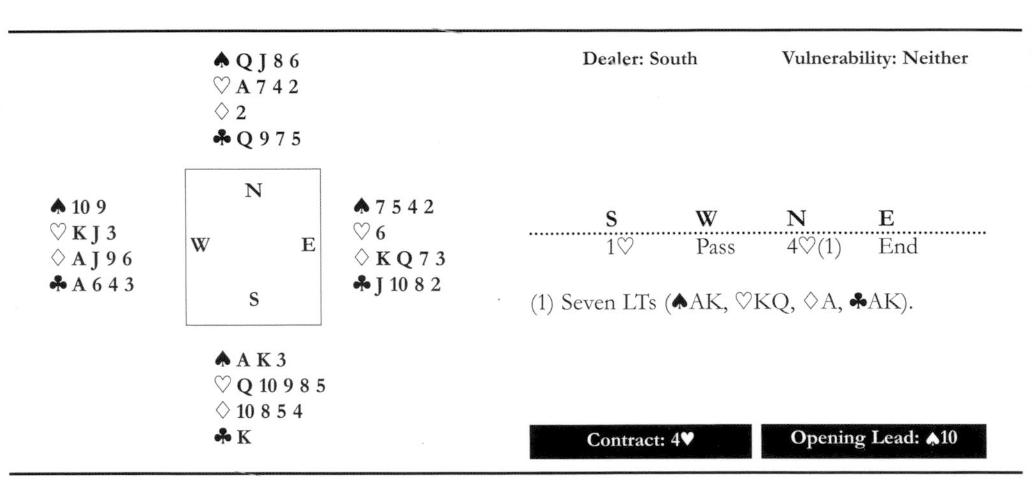

We will learn next page why a seven LT hand can raise a One-opener to Four - as on our deal.

There is a sneaky way to play the trump suit (missing ♡KJxx) that caters to either opponent holding ♡KJx. Lead low from the dummy, away from ♡Axxx. Only an expert East would play low from ♡Kx, so if East does play low, insert the ten; if this loses to the jack, later run the queen.

Declarer won the spade lead in dummy and led a low trump (key play) to the ten and jack. He won the spade return in hand (two rounds of diamonds - tough to find - would have been killing defence) and ran the queen of trumps, then leading a third trump to West's king and dummy's ace. He crossed to a third spade and led the king of clubs. The defence could win and play diamond - diamond, but declarer could ruff in dummy and discard his other two diamonds on the last spade winner and promoted queen of clubs. 10 tricks and game made.

Deal 6

The Losing Trick Count is a delightfully simple - and surprisingly accurate - method of hand evaluation if you have a four+ card fit with partner and an unbalanced hand (not so good if balanced).

STEP 1: Count up your Losing Tricks. Look at the first three cards of each suit; assume the ace takes the first round, the king the second and the queen the third. How many of those do you not have (up to the number of cards held)? Do this in each suit to obtain your total Losing Tricks (LTs).

STEP 2: Add your LTs to your partner's presumed number - if partner is an opener you should put them with seven LTs - and subtract the total from 18. Simply bid the answer!

Exercise: Partner opens 1♠. What do you bid with these:

(a)	(b)	(c)
♠ AQ82	♠ A1073	♠ QJ72
♡ 82	♡ 2	♡ Q2
◇ KJ942	◇ J94	◇ K9742
♣ 86	♣ KQ1082	♣ Q7

(a) STEP 1: You have seven LTs (♠K, ♡AK, ◇AQ, ♣AK). STEP 2: Add your seven to partner's presumed seven and subtract the total (14) from 18. Ergo - bid 4♠.

(b) STEP 1: You have seven LTs (♠KQ, ♡A, ◇AKQ, ♣A). STEP 2: Add your seven to partner's presumed seven and subtract the total (14) from 18. Ergo - bid 4♠.

(b) STEP 1: You have eight LTs (♠AK, ♡AK, ◇AQ, ♣AK). STEP 2: Add your eight to partner's presumed seven and subtract the total (15) from 18. Ergo - bid 3♠.

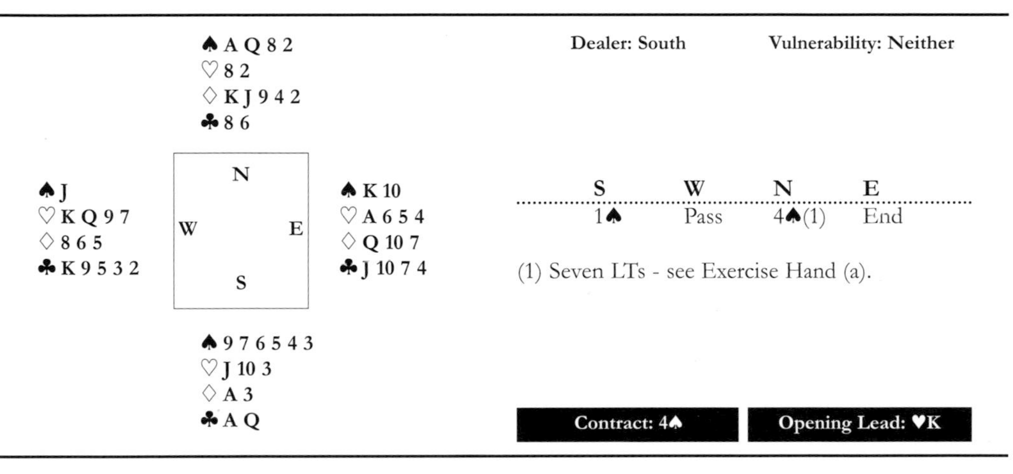

On our deal, West led the king of hearts vs 4♠, following with a low heart to East's ace, East switching to the jack of clubs. East had three possible finesses to take - the queen of trumps, jack of diamonds and (now) queen of clubs. How many do you think he took?

None. Declarer rose with the ace of clubs and sought to discard his club loser on a long diamond. He crossed to the ace of trumps in case the king was singleton (inferior odds than the finesse taking trumps in isolation - but he was not), then (both following with small trumps), crossed to the ace of diamonds, back to the king (no queen), then ruffed a third diamond. The suit split 3-3, whereupon he could ruff his third heart and lead a promoted fourth diamond, discarding his queen of clubs as East ruffed in with the king. 10 tricks and game made - with all three finesses destined to lose.

Deal 7

Here are the three criteria in which the Losing Trick Count LTC) operates:

Unbalanced hand - it is less accurate when 4333 (particularly so), 4432 and 5332.

Fit - four or more cards.

Opening side - normally you should not use it as the overcalling side - as you do not know how many Losing Tricks (LTs) with which to put partner.

By far the most important of the three is Fit. It is listed second only to enable a useful three-letter acronym memory aid: **UFO**.

Exercise: Will you use the LTC to determine the response to a 1♠ opener with these three hands?

(a)	(b)	(c)
♠ KJ73	♠ J952	♠ Q32
♡ AK2	♡ 2	♡ AJ84
◇ J42	◇ KQ843	◇ 4
♣ J62	♣ A108	♣ KJ872

(a). No - being balanced. You are worth 4♠ on high card points. Note that the LTC bid would be just 2♠ (nine LTs facing a presumed seven; subtracting the total from 18 gives 2♠). Clearly a nonsense given your point-count.

(b). Yes - satisfying 'UFO'. Holding seven LTs (♠AKQ, ♡A, ◇A, ♣KQ), you bid 4♠ [18 - (7+7)].

(c). No - lacking a four card fit. You are not going to support spades (at this stage), rather respond 2♣, your longest suit at the lowest level. If partner next rebids 2♡, you will use the LTC (seven LTs - ergo 4♡).

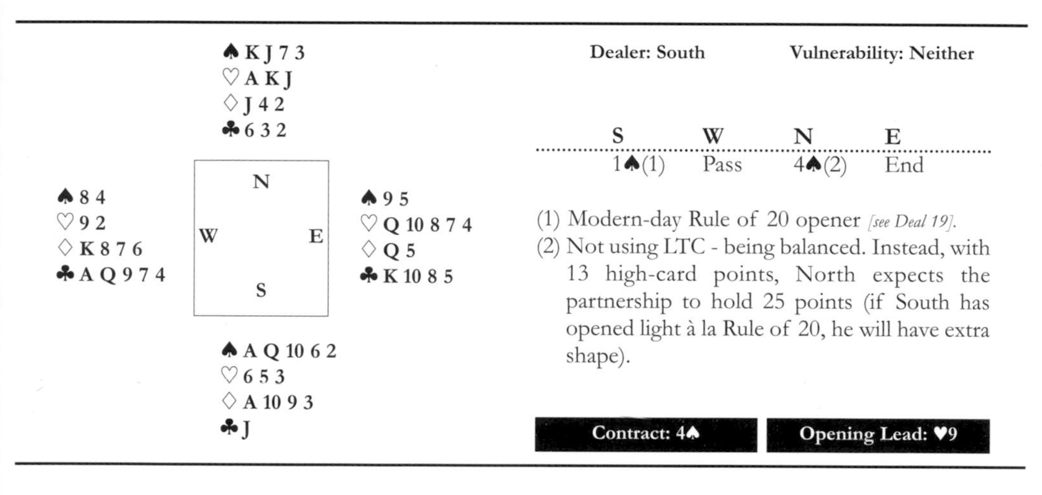

On our deal West's nine of hearts lead vs 4♠ almost certainly signified shortage. Rising with dummy's king, declarer immediately led a low diamond to the ten. West won the king and continued with the two of hearts.

Rising with the ace, declarer crossed to his ace of trumps and back to dummy's king (2-2 split - good). He then led a second low diamond, intending to finesse the nine. East's queen popped up, so he could win the ace, cross to the jack of diamonds, back to a third trump, cashed the nine of diamonds discarding the jack of hearts, ruffed his third heart, and merely conceded a club. 11 tricks and game made plus one.

Note declarer's care in diamonds, not squandering dummy's jack unnecessarily by leading it to either of the first two rounds.

Deal 8

You would open 1♠ with these:

(a)	(b)	(c)
♠ QJ962	♠ AQ753	♠ KQ8742
♡ 97	♡ K2	♡ A
♢ Q2	♢ AJ82	♢ KJ102
♣ KQJ2	♣ 73	♣ KQ

Say partner jumps to 3♠. What would you bid next?

The key is to understand what partner is saying: that 3♠ will be the limit facing a minimum - i.e. a seven Losing Trick (LT) opener. For each fewer LT you have, you should go up an extra level.

With (a), you have seven LTs (♠AK, ♡AK, ♢AK, ♣A). No better than advertised, you pass 3♠.

With (b) you have six LTs (♠K, ♡A, ♢KQ, ♣AK). One better than advertised, you go up to 4♠.

With (c) you have four LTs (♠A, ♢AQ, ♣A). Three better than advertised, you plan to bid to 6♠. It costs nothing, however, to check up in aces via the Blackwood 4NT ace-ask. Assuming partner has two aces (a 5♡ reply), you will bid 6♠.

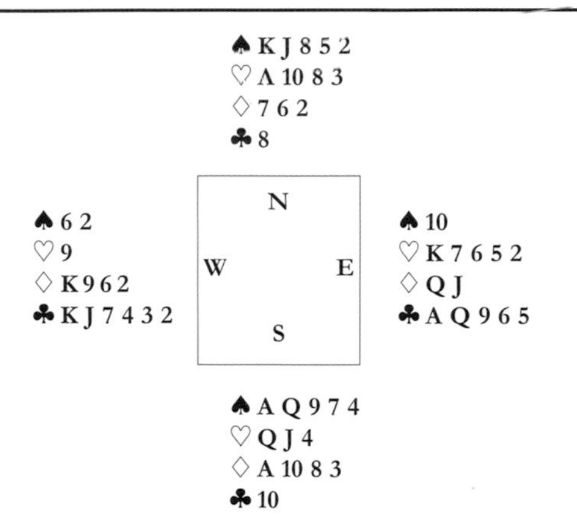

Dealer: South **Vulnerability: E-W**

S	W	N	E
1♠	Pass	3♠(1)	Pass(2)
4♠(3)	End		

(1) Eight LTs - in effect saying, 'Partner, this is our limit if you have your seven LTs, your expected minimum'.
(2) Put off by the vulnerability.
(3) One fewer LT (six) than the seven presumed, so goes up one extra level.

Contract: 4♠ **Opening Lead: ♥9**

4♠ on our deal was a decent enough game, largely depending on the position of the king of hearts. West's nine of hearts lead marked that card with East, however, and after wisely (or he'd have suffered two ruffs) rising with dummy's ace (and unblocking the jack), South's task looked hopeless.

Declarer drew trumps in two rounds, East throwing a club, then led the queen of hearts, East ducking his king (best). Winning the third heart, East again defended well by cashing the ace of clubs (or declarer's club would go on dummy's fourth heart) then switching to the queen of diamonds. Declarer won the ace, crossed to a third trump (East letting go a heart...?) and threw a diamond on dummy's winning heart. He then led a diamond, hoping for a miracle.

He got one. East's bare jack of diamonds won the trick (West could not afford to overtake), whereupon East's club return allowed declarer to ruff in one hand and discard the losing diamond from the other. 10 tricks and game made.

Did you spot East's missed chance? He needed to jettison the jack of diamonds as declarer crossed to a third trump. Now West must score ♢K9 - down one.

Deal 9

The Losing Trick Count may not always give the correct answer, but it is a more accurate method of evaluation than high-card points when you have a fit with partner and an unbalanced hand.

Work out how many Losing Tricks (LTs) you have; add partner's presumed number (this page's focus); then subtract the total from 18, bidding the answer.

We have learnt to put an opening bidder with seven LTs - what a typical minimum opener will contain. Here are three:

♠ AQ632	♠ A3	♠ K2
♡ KJ97	♡ QJ962	♡ A84
♢ Q2	♢ J974	♢ KJ9742
♣ J6	♣ K8	♣ J3

If you opened 1♠/1♡/1♢ respectively and partner raised to 3♠/3♡/3♢, you would pass with all three. Partner's bid is effectively saying that Three will be the limit assuming you have those seven LTs. For each LT fewer (i.e. better), you'd go up an extra level.

Now let's take a different (uncontested) auction: 1♢ - 1♠ - ? What now with these openers?

(a)	(b)	(c)
♠ KJ32	♠ AQ93	♠ KQJ2
♡ 97	♡ 2	♡ AJ8
♢ AQJ62	♢ AK874	♢ KQ942
♣ 86	♣ J98	♣ 8

You can use the LTC (four+ card support, unbalanced) but how many LTs do you presume partner for? He is not an opener - indeed he may have just six points - so cannot be put with seven LTs. Experience has shown that a typical minimum response at the One-level contains nine LTs.

With Hand (a) you bid 2♠ [you have seven LTs, added to partner's presumed nine and the total taken from 18]. With Hand (b) you bid 3♠ (six LTs facing a presumed nine). With hand (c) you bid 4♠ (five LTs facing nine).

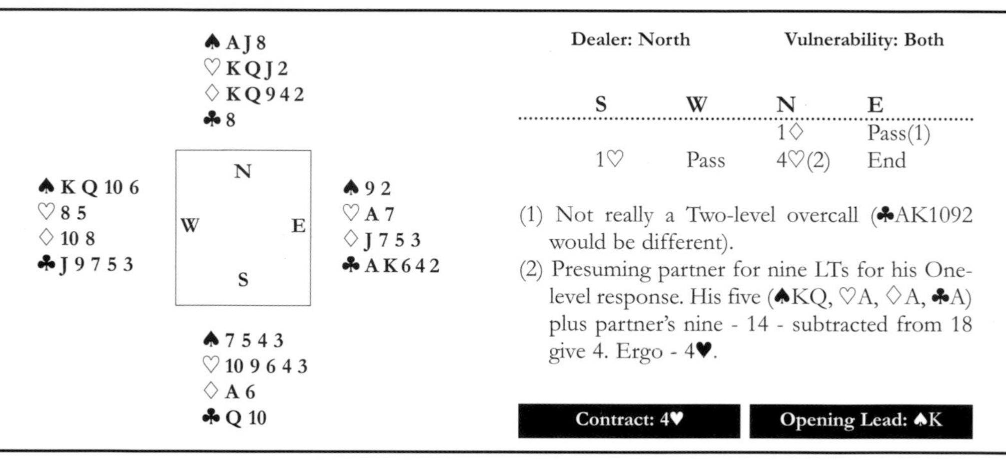

Dealer: North Vulnerability: Both

S	W	N	E
		1♢	Pass(1)
1♡	Pass	4♡(2)	End

(1) Not really a Two-level overcall (♣AK1092 would be different).

(2) Presuming partner for nine LTs for his One-level response. His five (♠KQ, ♡A, ♢A, ♣A) plus partner's nine - 14 - subtracted from 18 give 4. Ergo - 4♥.

Contract: 4♥ **Opening Lead: ♠K**

Had declarer - in his 4♡ - won the king of spades lead, he would have gone down. East wins the first trump, leads his second spade and receives a third-round ruff (plus the ace of clubs). Reasoning that West was more likely to hold four spades than five (no 1♠ overcall), declarer ducked the king of spades (key play). He won the second spade with dummy's jack and led a trump, but now there was no way for East to reach his partner's hand for the spade ruff (fortunately East held both ♣AK). Game made.

Deal 10

When using the Losing Trick Count (LTC), you presume partner for a number of Losing Tricks (LTs). Put an opener with seven, a One-over-One responder with nine and (new info.) a Two-over-One responder with eight

In tabulated form:

Partner's role	Approx min. high-card pts	LTs presumed
Opener	12	7
2/1 Resp.	9	8
1/1 Resp.	6	9

Exercise: You open 1♡ and partner responds 2◇. What next with:

(a)	(b)	(c)
♠ Q 2	♠ 3	♠ Q 2
♡ A K 8 7 3	♡ A Q J 7 2	♡ A K J 8 4
◇ Q J 4 2	◇ K 9 7 4 3	◇ K Q 4 3 2
♣ 9 6	♣ Q 8	♣ 7

(a) 3◇. You have seven LTs (♠AK, ♡Q, ◇AK, ♣AK); put partner with eight for his Two-over-One response; subtracting the total from 18 gives 3◇ - sensible given your minimal values.

(b) 4◇ - six LTs facing a presumed eight.

(c) 5◇ - 5 LTs. Playing Splinters (recommended) a 4♣ bid is best, showing a game raise in diamonds with short clubs. You can now play in 4♡ if partner bids it.

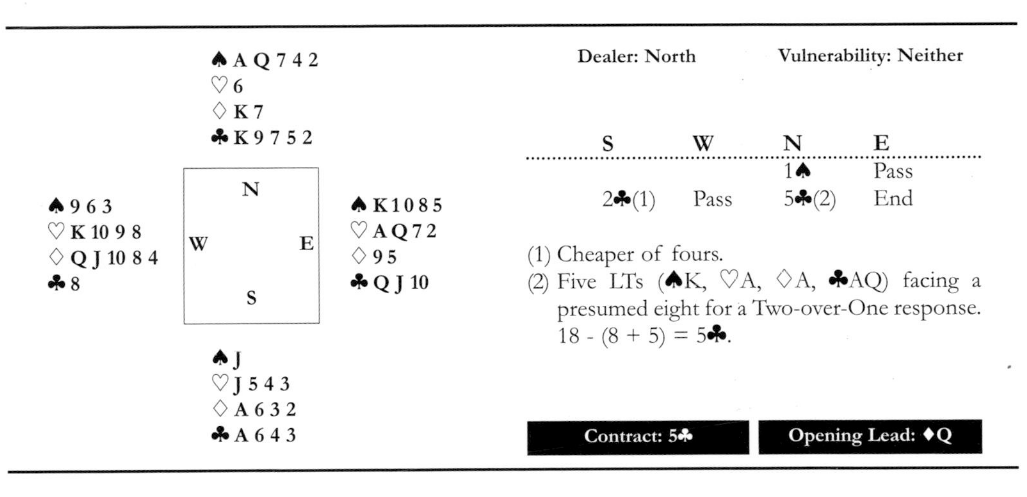

West led a normal queen of diamonds vs 5♣ - the only winning lead of the singleton trump being an impossibility to find. There was still much work for declarer to do.

Declarer won the ace of diamonds in order to lead the jack of spades, perhaps tempting a cover should West hold the king (and wanting to preserve the king of diamonds in dummy as a later entry). When West played a bored low spade, declarer wisely went up with dummy's ace, then ruffing a spade and giving up a heart. West won and switched to his trump (best).

Declarer won the trump with his ace, crossed to the king of diamonds, ruffed a third spade (both following but no king appearing), ruffed a heart, then ruffed a fourth spade with his last trump. If West had been able to overruff, the last defensive trump would have fallen under dummy's king (assuming no trump promotion). In fact declarer's trump held the trick, so he ruffed a third heart, cashed the king of trumps (West discarding), then followed with the long spade. All East could score was his master trump - 11 tricks and game made.

Deal 11

Partner opens 1♡ and you respond 1♠ with these four hands:

(a)	(b)	(c)	(d)
♠J9742	♠QJ93	♠A9632	♠AQ852
♡62	♡62	♡7	♡4
◇Q4	◇A4	◇K1092	◇KJ2
♣K852	♣J10852	♣QJ6	♣K752

The Losing Trick Count is not uppermost in your mind as you bid 1♠ - it will not figure unless partner supports you. However let us say partner now bids 3♠. Time to get into LTC mode.

Your partner will have presumed you for nine Losing Tricks (LTs) for your One-over-One response. For each fewer LT (than nine) you actually have, you should go up a level.

(a) You have nine LTs - nothing better than promised. Pass 3♠.

(b) Eight LTs - up to 4♠.

(c) Seven LTs. The LTC suggests you can make two higher levels - 5♠ - but there is no point bidding Five. Bid a confident 4♠.

(d) Six LTs - three better than advertised. You expect to make three levels higher than Three i.e. Six, but it costs you nothing to check up on aces via 4NT (if you are playing Roman Key Card Blackwood such that ♠K counts as an ace, so much the better).

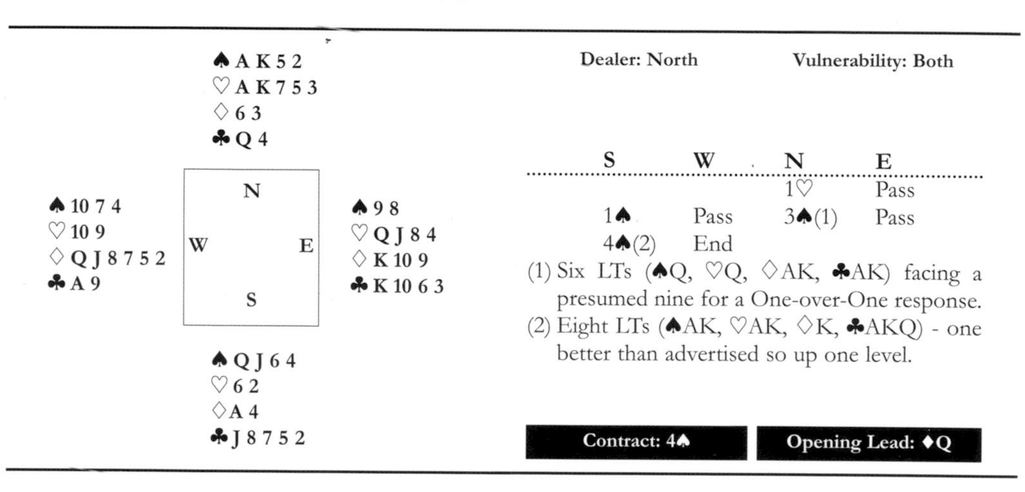

Declaring 4♠ on our deal, South won the queen of diamonds lead and correctly began setting up hearts. He crossed to the ace-king and led a third heart, East following high. Key moment.

Ruffing low would lead to an immediate demise - West overruffing and the defence cashing a diamond and two clubs. Ruffing high works no better, however, as a defence of leading trumps at each subsequent opportunity will leave declarer short (try it).

The only winning play, found at the table, is to discard the diamond (a loser in any event), West also throwing a diamond. East tried to cash the king of diamonds (a trump is best but declarer can still prevail by winning in hand and playing on clubs). Declarer ruffed, cashed the queen of trumps, led a low trump to the king, ruffed a fourth heart with the jack, then gave up two club tricks. He was able to ruff the opposing minor-suit lead at Trick 11, cash the ace of trumps drawing West's last trump then enjoy the long heart. Game made.

Deal 12

Let us review the LTC.

When to Use - 'UFO'

Unbalanced hands - it does not work so well with 5332, 4432 and (especially) 4333.
Fit - four+ cards with partner.
Opening side (so you know how many LTs to put partner with.

How to Use

Step 1: Count up LTs - look at how many of the ace (first round), king (second round), queen (third round) you do not hold, up to the number of cards held. e.g. *Ax* (1), *Qx* (2), *Jxxx* (3).

Step 2. Presume partner for a number of L… Opener - 7 LTs; Two-over-One respond… (e.g. 1♡ - 2♢) - 8 LTs; One-over-One respond… (e.g. 1♡ - 1♠) - 9 LTs.

Step 3. Add your LTs to partner's presumed LTs and subtract the total from 18. Bid the answer!

Question for the curious: Why 18?

Answer: The most LTs you can have is 12 (three in each suit); the most the partnership can hold is 24. Take six from 24 (tricks you are presumed to win before bidding begins) - 18.

North
♠ Q 3
♡ A Q 10 9 2
♢ A 8 7 5 4
♣ Q

West
♠ J 10 8 4
♡ K J 6
♢ Q J 9
♣ A 10 4

East
♠ K 9 7 6 2
♡ 8 5 3
♢ -
♣ J 9 7 5 3

South
♠ A 5
♡ 7 4
♢ K 10 6 3 2
♣ K 8 6 2

Dealer: North **Vulnerability: Neither**

S	W	N	E
		1♡	Pass
2♢	Pass	4♢(1)	Pass
5♢(2)	End		

(1) Six LTs (♠AK, ♡K, ♢KQ, ♣A) facing a presumed eight (Two-over-One responder). 18 - (8 + 6) = 4♢.
(2) One fewer LT than the eight advertised (♠K, ♡AK, ♢AQ, ♣AQ), so up one level.

Contract: 5♦ **Opening Lead: ♠J**

This page's deal saw declarer - in 5♢ - try dummy's queen of spades on West's jack, but had to win his ace when East in turn covered with the king. When at Trick two declarer cashed the king of trumps (preserving dummy's ace), he saw East discard.

With three losers staring him in the face (a spade, a trump and the ace of clubs), declarer needed something good to happen in hearts. He led low to the queen (winning), then cashed the ace on which West dropped the king. He now led the ten, East playing low. Should he play West for an original ♡Kx - now throwing a spade - or ♡KJx (and have made the good and correct play of the king from his equals the previous round - the card he was known to hold)?

The point is that if East held ♡Jxxx, he would have covered the ten to prevent a quick discard. Declarer therefore ruffed the third heart and duly brought down West's jack. He now crossed to the ace of trumps and threw his spade loser on a long heart. All the defence scored were their master trump and ace of clubs. 11 tricks and game made - adroit work.

Deal 13

The Losing Trick Count is not a convention, like Blackwood. You do not need to ask a new partner, 'Do you play the LTC?' Rather, it is a method of hand evaluation to make your bidding judgement better in those situations in which it is appropriate to use LTC (i.e. fit situations when holding four+ card support in an unbalanced hand).

You should still use the LTC even if partner isn't; perhaps he isn't because he doesn't use it (you could always teach him...) or because his hand is balanced (you would not know this).

On our featured deal we see a player using high-card points (North - being balanced) in conjunction with a player using the LTC (South). The correct contract was reached - ostensibly a 75% 4♡ needing one club honour onside (i.e. with East).

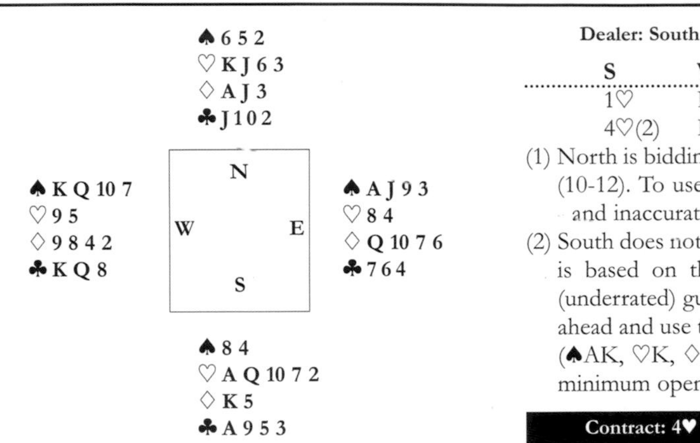

Dealer: South **Vulnerability: Neither**

S	W	N	E
1♡	Pass	3♡(1)	Pass
4♡(2)	End		

(1) North is bidding 3♡ based on his point-count (10-12). To use the LTC would be misguided and inaccurate - being balanced.

(2) South does not know whether North's 3♡ bid is based on the LTC, high-card points, or (underrated) gut-feel. However he can still go ahead and use the LTC: holding one fewer LT (♠AK, ♡K, ◇A, ♣KQ) than the seven of a minimum opener, he goes up a level.

Contract: 4♥ **Opening Lead: ♠K**

West led the king of spades, East encouraging with the nine and continued with a second spade to East's ace. At Trick Three East blithely led a third spade (switching to a club would have been better). Declarer ruffed the spade and cashed the ace of trumps. Seeking to improve his odds from 75%, declarer now eliminated diamonds - king, over to the ace, ruff the jack - then led a second trump to the jack.

Declarer was delighted to observe the 2-2 trump split, for his game was now secure. He ran the jack of clubs in the five-card ending *(see across)*. West won the queen but was endplayed.

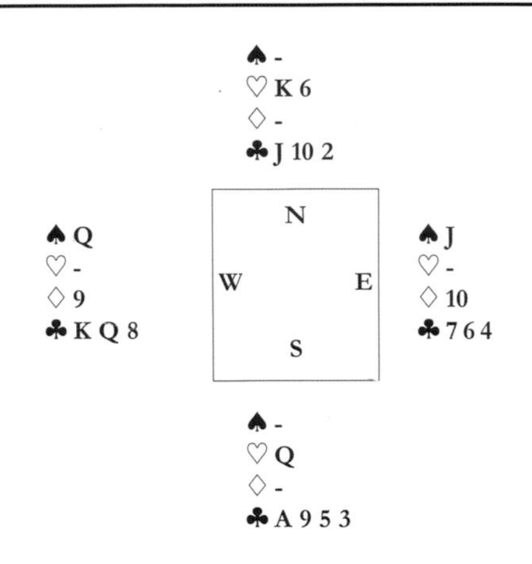

A club from the king would prevent a second loser, but West's choice of a spade enabled declarer to throw a club from dummy and ruff in hand. 10 tricks and game made.

Deal 14

The LTC works equally well for minors as majors.

Exercise: 1♢ - ?

(a) ♠ 9 3
♡ 10 2
♢ K J 7 6
♣ K J 10 8 2

(b) ♠ 2
♡ K J 7
♢ Q 9 4 2 3
♣ A J 7 6

(c) ♠ K 6
♡ A J 8 4 2
♢ K J 4 2
♣ 7 5

(a) 3♢. Eight LTs facing opener's presumed seven. Subtracting the total from 18 gives 3♢.

(b) 4♢. Seven LTs facing opener's presumed seven.

(c) 1♡. Better to introduce the major. You can always support diamonds later (using the LTC - 3♢ will be your supporting bid).

Exercise: 1♢ - 3♢ - ?

(d) ♠ K 8 6
♡ 3
♢ A Q 9 8 4 2
♣ A Q 2

(e) ♠ 2
♡ A K 5 3
♢ A Q 9 4 3 2
♣ A 6

(f) ♠ K 6
♡ K 4
♢ A Q 9 7 4 2
♣ Q J 5

(d) 5♢. Two fewer LTs than the seven advertised - go up two levels. Compare with responder's hand (a) - 5♢ is a good contract.

(e) 6♢. Three fewer LTs - up three levels. Compare with (a) above and you'll see that 6♢ is almost certain to make.

(f) 3NT. With no shortage plus stoppers in all suits, the nine-trick notrump game should be easier than the 11-trick diamond game.

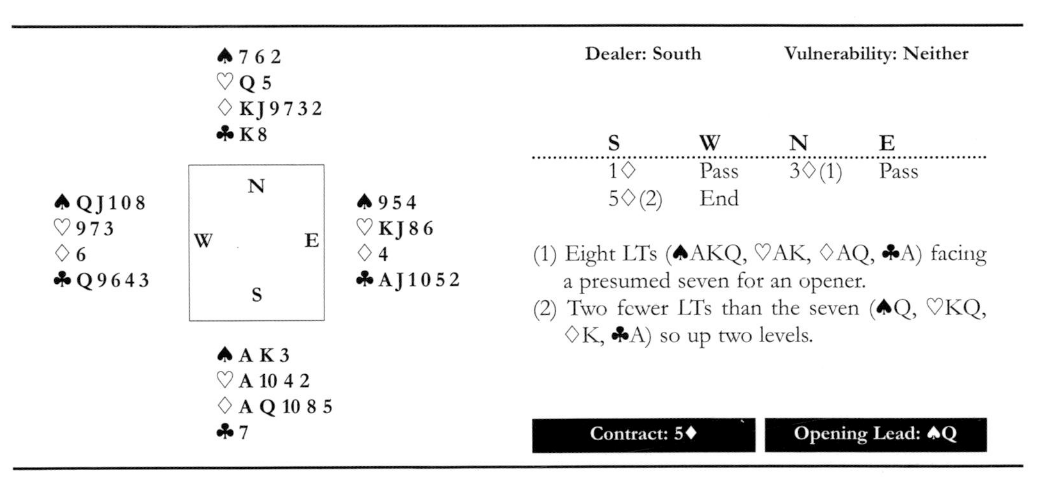

On our deal West led the queen of spades vs 5♢ and declarer was in danger of losing a spade, a heart and the ace of clubs. One possibility was to lead up to the king of clubs - if West held the ace then, even if he played it, dummy's king would provide a discard for declarer's third spade. However if the king lost to East's ace and a spade came back, declarer would be too late to do anything with hearts.

Better was to start on hearts, not clubs, for hearts gave him two chances (as you'll see). Declarer won the spade, drew trumps and led a heart to the queen. Had West held the king (and say played it), declarer could win a spade return, cross to the promoted queen of hearts, back to a trump, then discard a spade on the ace of hearts.

In fact dummy's queen of hearts lost to East's king. Declarer won East's spade, crossed to dummy in trumps, then tried Chance No. 2 - a heart to his ten. The finesse against the jack was successful and he could now discard dummy's third spade on his ace of hearts. He merely gave up a club. 11 tricks and game made.

Deal 15

Is the LTC always accurate? No - it may be more accurate than high-card points in fit situations (with unbalanced hands); but how can a method that evaluates these two hands below (in response to a 1♠ opener) as the same 4♠ bid be foolproof:

(a)		(b)	
♠	Q 9 6 4 2	♠	A J 6 4 2
♡	5 2	♡	Q 2
◇	Q 9 7 5 2	◇	A J 7 5 2
♣	3	♣	K

Evaluating queens the same as aces (in suits of three+ cards) is clearly inaccurate. Some (e.g. the excellent Australian teacher Ron Klinger) recommend making adjustments: e.g. a holding of Qxx needs a compensating ace to avoid being three losers.

Whilst very much agreeing with the inaccuracies of the LTC, I will not be going the adjustment route. Firstly, let's keep things simple; secondly, make too many adjustments and it is like shaving table legs to try to make it flat - sometimes you end up with no legs at all; thirdly I do not want us ultimately to be a slave to the LTC. Use it as an initial guide, but then consider other factors. Factors to which we will be devoting the rest of our series.

Don't get me wrong. I do like the LTC, but ten pages of seeing it work perfectly may have given you the impression it always works. So, to correct that misapprehension...

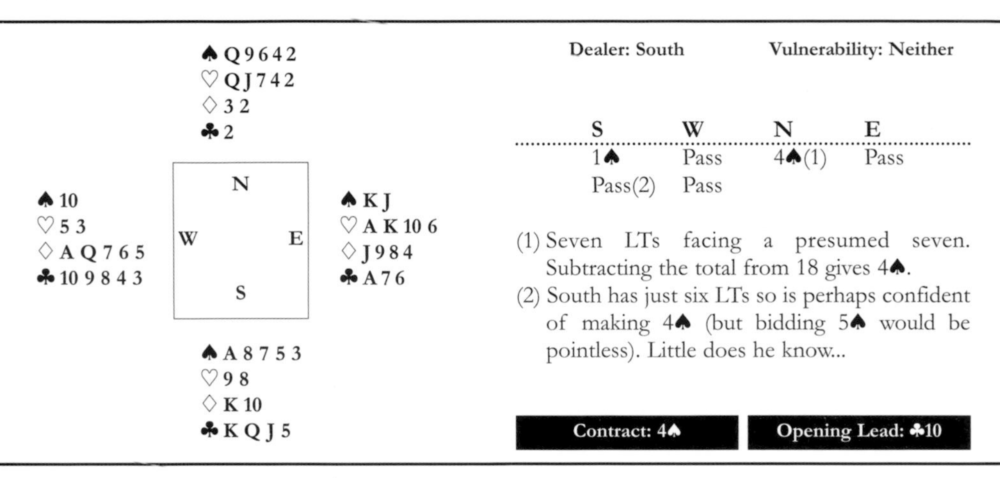

North: ♠ Q 9 6 4 2 ♡ Q J 7 4 2 ◇ 3 2 ♣ 2

West: ♠ 10 ♡ 5 3 ◇ A Q 7 6 5 ♣ 10 9 8 4 3

East: ♠ K J ♡ A K 10 6 ◇ J 9 8 4 ♣ A 7 6

South: ♠ A 8 7 5 3 ♡ 9 8 ◇ K 10 ♣ K Q J 5

Dealer: South **Vulnerability: Neither**

S	W	N	E
1♠	Pass	4♠(1)	Pass
Pass(2)	Pass		

(1) Seven LTs facing a presumed seven. Subtracting the total from 18 gives 4♠.

(2) South has just six LTs so is perhaps confident of making 4♠ (but bidding 5♠ would be pointless). Little does he know...

Contract: 4♠ **Opening Lead: ♣10**

West led the ten of clubs vs 4♠, a contract in which the LTC would calculate that an overtrick would be made. East won the ace and switched to a diamond. Declarer tried the king, but West won the ace and cashed the queen. At Trick Four he switched to the five of hearts.

East beat dummy's jack of hearts with the king, cashed the ace, then led a third heart (to rub salt into the wound). Ruffing with the ace would see East's ♠KJ promoted into two tricks, so declarer discarded. West ruffed with his singleton ten and East had to come to a further trump trick.

Declarer was down four, making five fewer tricks than the LTC would suggest. An extreme example - yes - but you get the point. Enjoy the LTC - it will surely help your Bridge - but don't think it's gospel.

Deal 16

Bidding and play may be connected. However your point-count and Losing Trick Count, guides for bidding, have no intrinsic value once play begins.

Which dummy would you prefer to table after this (uncontested) bidding: 1♡ - 1♠ - 2◇ - 2♡ - 4♡?

a) ♠ KQ742
♡ 432
◇ 874
♣ QJ

(b) ♠ 86432
♡ QJ2
◇ K2
♣ 862

Decided? Here is partner's hand:

c) ♠ 5
♡ AK9765
◇ AQJ3
♣ 10 9

Hand (b) is superb - all your points in partner's suits make 4♡ a cinch (six heart tricks and four diamonds).

Hand (a) - yuk! No points in partner's suits, and not even the ace of either black suit, facing the known shortage. Imagine playing 4♡ after the defence cash the ace-king of clubs and ace of spades before switching to a trump. Even on 2-2 trumps, 4♡ won't make unless the king of diamonds is singleton (no dummy entry - look at your heart spots). On a 3-1 trump split and 4-2 diamond split, partner will be held to just seven tricks.

By the way, what do you think of partner's jump to 4♡? It was certainly a stretch - given that your 2♡ was a mere preference bid, not actual support, in a 6-9 point hand, and often based on a doubleton heart. Had he made the sounder invitational raise to 3♡, you'd have passed in a flash with (a) and raised to 4♡ (in the same flash) with (b). I hardly need point out that (a) contains two more high-card points than (b).

North:
♠ J 8 6 3 2
♡ Q 10
◇ Q J
♣ 8 6 3 2

West:
♠ K Q 10 4
♡ A 7 5
◇ 9 4 2
♣ Q 9 4

East:
♠ A 9 7
♡ 8 4
◇ 10 8 7 6
♣ A 10 7 5

South:
♠ 5
♡ K J 9 6 3 2
◇ A K 5 3
♣ K J

Dealer: West Vulnerability: Neither

S	W	N	E
	Pass	Pass	Pass
1♡	Pass	1♠	Pass
2◇(1)	Pass	2♡	Pass
3♡	Pass	4♡(2)	End

(1) Correct to introduce the cheaper four-card side-suit than repeating the six.
(2) Few points, but loves his red-suits.

Contract: 4♥ **Opening Lead: ♠K**

On our deal West led king and a second spade. Declarer ruffed, led a trump to the queen, then the ten, losing to West's ace who returned a passive third trump (best).

Declarer crossed to the queen of diamonds and led a club (East playing low), facing the dreaded king-jack guess. Except that it was no guess because West, a passed hand, had shown the king-queen of spades and ace of hearts. No room for the ace of clubs - so declarer rose with the king and made 4♡ for the loss of a spade, a heart and a club. With just 21 points.

Deal 17

Your mantra when bidding should be *'Think Tricks not Points'*.

Exercise: Which of these hands should bid 2♢ as an overcall over an opposing 1♡ opener?

(a)	(b)	(c)
♠ 6 2	♠ 3	♠ K J 2
♡ Q 8 5	♡ 6 2	♡ A J 4
♢ A K 7 4 2	♢ K J 10 9 6 2	♢ A Q 6 3 2
♣ K J 6	♣ K Q 8 5	♣ 10 7

Try the 'sick as a parrot' test. If you are left to play there (doubled?), do you feel sick as a parrot?

Hand (a). You would certainly feel sick as a parrot if declaring 2♢ (doubled): no diamond filling and no tricks. On a bad day you could make just two or three tricks - and - worse - find that your defensive strength prevents the opponents from even being able to make a game. Pass over 1♡. Don't bid 2♢.

Hand (b). You would be pretty happy to be left in 2♢ (doubled). You have little defence to opposing contracts and are bound to garner six or seven tricks facing next-to-nothing. Playing the Weak Jump Overcall (recommended) you might even try 3♢.

Hand (c). Like (a), your hand is better suited to defence. However your point-count is so good that you don't want to be talked out of a game on sheer high-card power. That game will surely be 3NT, so rather than bidding 2♢ on that anaemic suit, bid 1NT (15-19) with a stopper in the opposing hearts.

North: ♠ K J 10 7 ♡ 10 8 6 4 ♢ J 6 ♣ K 10 9

West: ♠ 9 3 ♡ 7 ♢ Q 10 9 8 3 ♣ Q J 8 4 2

East: ♠ A Q 5 4 ♡ A Q 9 3 2 ♢ 5 ♣ A 7 5

South: ♠ 8 6 2 ♡ K J 5 ♢ A K 7 4 2 ♣ 6 3

Dealer: East **Vulnerability: Neither**

S	W	N	E
			1♡
2♢(1)	Pass	Pass	Dbl(2)
Pass(3)	Pass(4)	Pass	

(1) 'I'm only non-vulnerable'. Yuk - look at the absence of tricks. Plus, non-vulnerable doubled undertricks got more expensive in 1993 (300 per trick from down four onwards instead of 200).
(2) Reopening take-out double - far superior than 2♠ as events were about to show.
(3) Sick as a parrot.
(4) Delighted to convert to penalties.

Contract: 2♦Doubled **Opening Lead: ♥7**

On our deal, South's sick-as-a-parrot-test-failing overcall got its just desserts. East won the heart with the ace and returned the nine of hearts (a suit preference signal for the higher-ranking spades). West ruffed declarer's jack and duly returned the nine of spades to the ten and queen. A third heart was ruffed, then came a second spade to the ace and a spade, ruffed.

Declarer covered the queen of clubs that came next, but East beat dummy's king with the ace and returned the queen of hearts. West's remaining ♢Q10 of trumps was promoted (he overruffed declarer's low ruff) and cashed the jack of clubs. Down four, E-W 800, and a sick-as-a-parrot South.

At the other table the bidding was short: 1♡ - P - P - P!

Deal 18

Which of these hands would you rather hold in response to partner's 1NT opener?

(a) ♠ 8 6 2
♡ K 9 7
◇ Q 4 2
♣ A Q J 5

(b) ♠ 8 6 2
♡ K 9
◇ Q 4 2
♣ A Q J 5 2

(c) ♠ 8 2
♡ K 9
◇ 4 2
♣ A Q J 5 4 3 2

Hand (a) is a classic raise to 2NT. With no exciting features, the partnership will need a full 25/26 points to make 3NT. 3NT invites partner in the classic manner - minimum or maximum?

Hand (b) is worth a raise to 3NT. Yes - the partnership could be one point short of the 25-point game guideline, but the fifth club is probably worth a whole trick.

Hand (c) contains two points fewer but I'd have no hesitation jumping from 1NT to 3NT.

Give partner this 11-point hand (d) (not even enough to open 1NT), and 3NT will make half the time (i.e. when the club finesse works). Note that I'd not even contemplate bidding 5♣ over 1NT with (c) - 11 is bound to be too many tricks to win.

(d) ♠ Q J 9 3
♡ A 4 3
◇ Q J 9 3
♣ 10 6

Many teachers recommend adding points for length. I do not - in keeping with my desire to keep things simple. Further - whilst length is usually good, it can be neutral - or worse. If partner opens 1♡ and rebids 2◇ over your 1♠, you'd rather hold Hand (e) than (f):

(e) ♠ A 4 3 2
♡ J 9 2
◇ J 9 2
♣ A 3 2

(f) ♠ A 5 4 3 2
♡ J 9
◇ J 9
♣ A 4 3 2

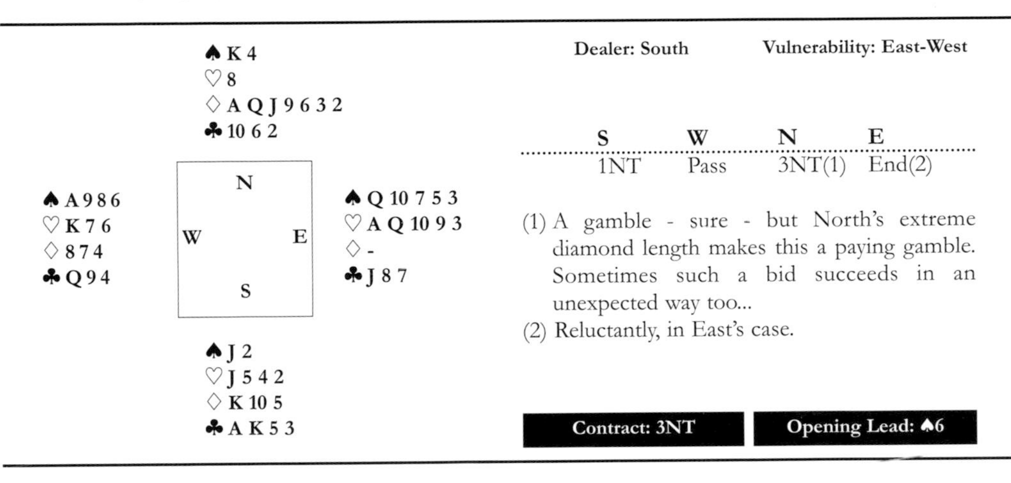

North: ♠ K 4 ♡ 8 ◇ A Q J 9 6 3 2 ♣ 10 6 2

West: ♠ A 9 8 6 ♡ K 7 6 ◇ 8 7 4 ♣ Q 9 4

East: ♠ Q 10 7 5 3 ♡ A Q 10 9 3 ◇ - ♣ J 8 7

South: ♠ J 2 ♡ J 5 4 2 ◇ K 10 5 ♣ A K 5 3

Dealer: South **Vulnerability: East-West**

S	W	N	E
1NT	Pass	3NT(1)	End(2)

(1) A gamble - sure - but North's extreme diamond length makes this a paying gamble. Sometimes such a bid succeeds in an unexpected way too...
(2) Reluctantly, in East's case.

Contract: 3NT **Opening Lead: ♠6**

Ascribing full value to the long suit on our deal, North leapt to 3NT and South faced an agonising guess on West's spade lead. However there was sound logic to his play of dummy's king: if East holds the ace of spades (and West the queen), even a winning guess of playing low in dummy, using the power of the jack in hand to force out East's ace, will not prevail - East will switch to hearts.

The king of spades winning Trick One, declarer quickly cashed seven diamond tricks and the ace-king of clubs. 10 tricks and game made plus one.

At the other table...North proceeded in a more circumspect manner, let E-W in (East doubled a diamond bid for take-out) and the resulting 4♠ contract proved unbeatable.

Deal 19

I will not be recommending adding points for length. Sometimes a long suit is more useful than others, so it is somewhat arbitrary to put a specific value on e.g. the fifth and sixth cards of a suit. However here is a guideline I recommend that does factor in length.

The Rule of 20

Open the bidding when the number of high-card points added to the number of cards in your two longest suits reaches 20.

(a)	(b)	(c)
♠ A J 8 3	♠ A 2	♠ Q J 10 3 2
♡ K 6 2	♡ K J 9 7 3	♡ 4
◇ 4	◇ Q 9 8 4 2	◇ 2
♣ K 10 8 4 2	♣ 6	♣ A Q 8 7 4 2
Open 1♣	Open 1♡	Open 1♣

It must be said, however, that the above three hands all have honours in their long suits, plus easy rebids. Here are two Rule-of-20-satisfying-hands that I would not open:

(d)	(e)
♠ Q 2	♠ K
♡ Q 8 5 2	♡ A J 2
◇ K J 8 5 2	◇ Q J 6 2
♣ Q J	♣ 8 6 4 3 2

Honours in short suits, no easy rebid - you are best passing both (d) and (e). In other words: use the Rule of 20 as a guide not a gospel.

North: ♠ A K 5 4 ♡ A 8 3 2 ◇ A 8 5 4 ♣ 3

West: ♠ 8 ♡ K Q J 10 ◇ J 9 6 3 ♣ K J 9 5

East: ♠ 9 7 6 ♡ 9 7 6 5 ◇ K Q 10 7 ♣ 10 6

South: ♠ Q J 10 3 2 ♡ 4 ◇ 2 ♣ A Q 8 7 4 2

Dealer: South **Vulnerability: Neither**

S	W	N	E
1♣(1)	Pass	1◇(2)	Pass
1♠	Pass	2♡(3)	Pass
2♠(4)	Pass	4NT(5)	Pass
5◇(6)	Pass	5♡(7)	Pass
6♠(8)	Pass	7♠(9)	end

(1) Satisfying the Rule of 20.
(2) Cheaper of Fours as responder.
(3) Fourth Suit Forcing. North seeks more information before deciding whether to play 4♠, 6♠ or even 7♠.
(4) Repeating the second suit to show five cards. Because South would open 1♠ with 5♠-5♣, he must now have six clubs.
(5) Roman Key Card Blackwood agreeing spades - North is ecstatic partner has 11 black cards (he has the two red aces as 'cover cards' for those two red cards).
(6) One or four of 'five aces' (incl. ♠K).
(7) Do you have ♠Q?
(8) Yes - but in theory no side-king (South would bid a side-king at the Six-level).
(9) Might pass - there'll be work in 7♠.

Contract: 7♠ **Opening Lead: ♥K**

In 7♠ declarer won the heart lead with dummy's ace, crossed to the ace of clubs and ruffed a club (low). He crossed to the ten of trumps, ruffed a third club (high), cashed the ace of diamonds, ruffed a diamond, ruffed a fourth club (with dummy's last - high - trump), ruffed a heart, drew East's two remaining trumps and ran his two long clubs. 13 tricks and grand slam made - with just 24 high-card points. West was left to rue that an opening trump lead would have effectively removed an entry to declarer's hand prematurely and rendered the grand slam unmakeable.

Deal 20

Be in no doubt: length is a huge asset in a Bridge hand. I may not be recommending adding points for a long suit, however it is factored into such guidelines I preach such as the Rule of 20 and - this page - the Rule of 14.

Rule of 14

Respond in a new suit at the Two-level after partner has opened One-of-a-Suit when the high-card points in your hand added to your longest suit gets to 14.

Exercise: Partner opens 1♡. What would you respond with:

(a)	(b)	(c)
♠ 42	♠ 942	♠ J 10 2
♡ J7	♡ J7	♡ J7
◇ QJ942	◇ QJ94	◇ QJ94
♣ AJ86	♣ AJ86	♣ AJ86

(a) Bid 2◇. Five diamonds and nine points make this a Rule-of-14-satisfying hand.

(b) 1NT. The Rule of 14 fails so content yourself with the Weak 6-9 point 'dustbin' 1NT response.

(c) 2♣. With 10+ points you always have enough strength to bid a new suit at the Two-level (no need to waste time applying the Rule of 14); prefer the cheaper of fours as responder.

And these (responding to 1♡)?...

(d)	(e)	(f)
♠ 432	♠ J842	♠ 42
♡ 7	♡ J7	♡ Q97
◇ KJ942	◇ Q9765	◇ Q9742
♣ A986	♣ K6	♣ A86

(d) 1NT. Fails the Rule of 14 and no better alternative than the 'dustbin' 1NT. Dustbin is as dustbin sounds - a last resort - so...

(e) 1♠. Always respond a higher-ranking four-card suit in preference to 1NT. A 1NT response to 1♡ categorically denies four spades.

(f) 2♡. Prefer the three-card raise (especially holding a picture card such as, here, ♡Q) to 1NT.

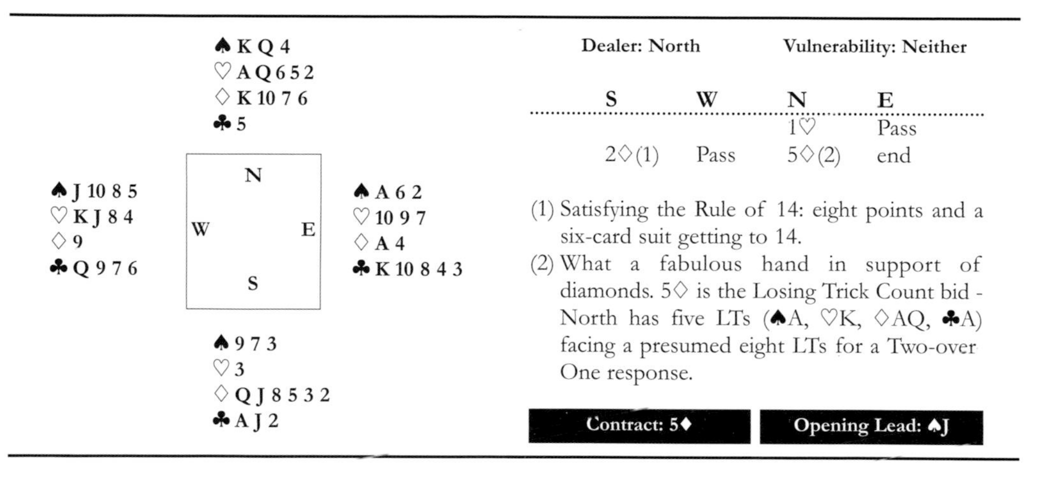

On our deal, declarer covered West's jack of spades lead with dummy's queen, East winning the ace and returning the six of spades for the seven and eight. Winning dummy's king, declarer needed to dump his third spade quickly.

Declarer crossed to the ace of clubs and took the necessary risk of a heart to the queen (phew - it held). He cashed the ace discarding a spade and could now lose just the ace of trumps. 11 tricks - game made.

Deal 21

Contrast these two hands:

(a) ♠ Q 2
♡ J 3 2
◇ A J 4 2
♣ K 4 3 2

(b) ♠ Q 9
♡ J 10 3
◇ A J 10 9
♣ K 10 8 3

Imagine partner opened 1NT. What would you respond?

The point-count response with both is an invitational 2NT. I would bid 2NT with neither. Hand (a) is so grotty I'd pass in a flash - nine tricks look an awfully long way away facing a flat 12-14. Yet I'd bid 3NT with Hand (b) in spite of having the same top cards and the same shape. The difference: *intermediates.*

Some schools advocate adding half a point for a ten. I prefer not to go there - on simplicity grounds and also because some tens (e.g. in short-suits or in opposing suits) are worth less, whilst others (e.g. adjoining a jack/nine and/or in notrumps) are worth more. However whilst tens and nines do not count as points, they sure are useful.

Say the 1NT opener holds:

♠ J 10 4 3
♡ A 5 4
◇ Q 7 3
♣ A Q 5

You would be struggling to make 1NT (on a heart lead) facing Hand (a) above. Yet 3NT would have good chances facing (b)...

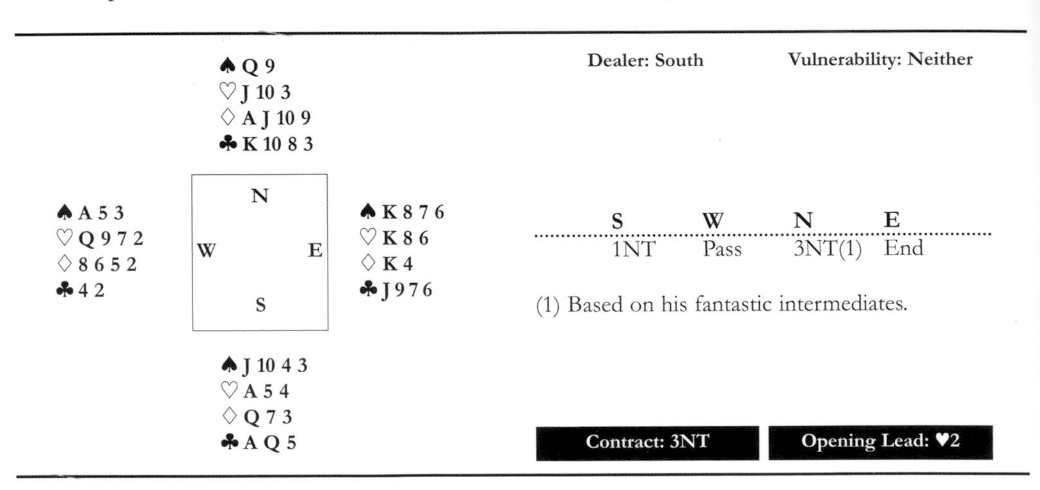

Trick One went ♡2, ♡10, ♡K and declarer won the ace immediately, knowing dummy's jack would provide a second stopper. Correctly playing the suit in which he had certain losers and could promote two sure tricks using the four-card sequence, declarer led a spade to the queen at Trick Two.

East won the king and returned the eight of hearts which passed to dummy's ten. Declarer led the nine of spades next, West winning the ace and cashing his promoted queen-nine of hearts (East throwing a spade and declarer and dummy both throwing diamonds).

West now switched to the eight of diamonds but, judging the king was offside and hoping for four club tricks, declarer rose with dummy's ace. He crossed to the ace-queen of clubs (no jack), then cashed the promoted jack-ten of spades. throwing diamonds from dummy. East was squeezed on the second - forced to throw from ♣J9 or release his king of diamonds. Either was fatal, making West wish he'd switched to a diamond *before* cashing the hearts (no squeeze). Nine tricks and game made.

Deal 22

Contrast (i) *K32* facing *Q54* and
(ii) *432* facing *KQ5*.

In (i) you can only win one trick barring a miracle. In (ii) you will win a second trick half the time - when the ace is sitting in front of (i.e. playing before) the KQ5.

Similarly Q32 facing J54 will probably not yield a trick when the opposing ace and king are split, yet 432 facing QJ5 will provide a trick unless both the ace and king are sitting over (i.e. playing after) the QJ5.

It is the sequential nature of the KQ5 and QJ5 that make them so powerful. Make QJ5 into KQJ5 or QJ105 and it is all the more powerful.

Sequential holdings are hugely lucrative - and are normally worth well beyond their high-card point value. Contrast:

(a)	(b)
♠ Q 8 2	♠ Q J 3
♡ A 10	♡ A 2
◇ K J 6 4	◇ K Q 6 4
♣ Q 9 3 2	♣ 10 9 8 2

Both have an ace, a king, two queens, a jack, a ten, a nine and an eight. Both have the same shape. Yet Hand (b) is much more powerful in terms of likely trick-taking. It has three sequential holdings (♠QJ, ◇KQ, ♣1098) whilst Hand (a) has none. If partner opened 1NT, you'd scrape up a 2NT bid with a heavy heart holding (a), yet jump to 3NT unhesitatingly with (b). The wisdom of which is seen...

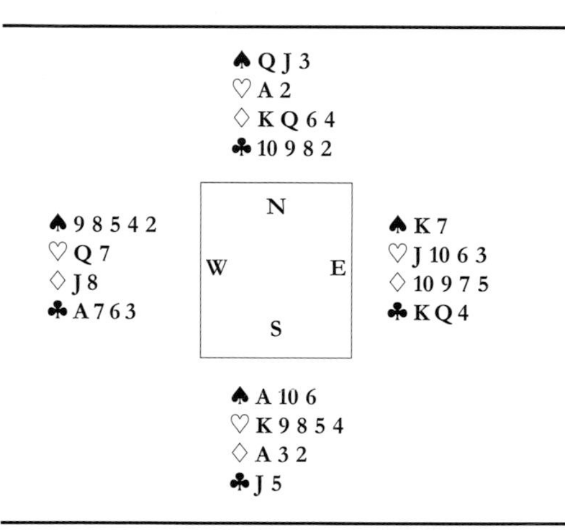

Dealer: South **Vulnerability: Neither**

S	W	N	E
1NT(1)	Pass	3NT(2)	End

(1) Opening 1NT avoids the need for a rebid - unlike opening 1♡.
(2) Look at the sequences.

Contract: 3NT **Opening Lead: ♠9**

Trick One went ♠9, ♠J, ♠K, ♠A and declarer began developing the one suit at Trick Two which would lead to success. Which one?

Clubs. Rather than rely on an against-the-odds 3-3 red-suit split, declarer instead used the four-card club sequence to drive out the three opposing top cards and so promoted the fourth. The jack of clubs rode to East's queen, a spade coming back. Declarer won his ten and led a second club to East's king. Declarer won the three of hearts with dummy's ace and led the ten of clubs to West's ace. He won West's third spade in dummy and could now triumphantly cash the promoted nine of clubs, emerging with a tenth trick when East was forced to unguard hearts or (his actual choice) throw a diamond. Ten tricks and game made plus one.

Moral: upgrade sequences in the bidding, then utilise them in the play.

Deal 23

As we have seen, three of the most important factors in evaluating a Bridge hand - aside from high-card points - are...

Length
Intermediates
Sequences

As an aide-memoire for the three-letter acronym 'LIS', try 'Living In Sin'.

Exercise: You open 1NT with these four hands and partner invites game with 2NT. With which would you accept the invite?

(a)	(b)	(c)	(d)
♠KJ4	♠62	♠QJ2	♠Q3
♡Q87	♡QJ2	♡A4	♡KJ76
◇J42	◇AQ974	◇K1093	◇A102
♣AQ52	♣A52	♣QJ105	♣K632

Hand (b) with its five-card diamond suit and Hand (c) with its sequential holdings (◇109 and ♣10 could make all the difference) should bid 3NT. Note that you are worried about spades on Hand (b) but it's better to have good suits and a commensurately weak suit rather than the jam too thinly spread - as on Hands (a) and (d). The other two [(a) and (d)] are unlikely to yield nine tricks - especially that yukky intermediate and sequence-free 4333 Hand (a).

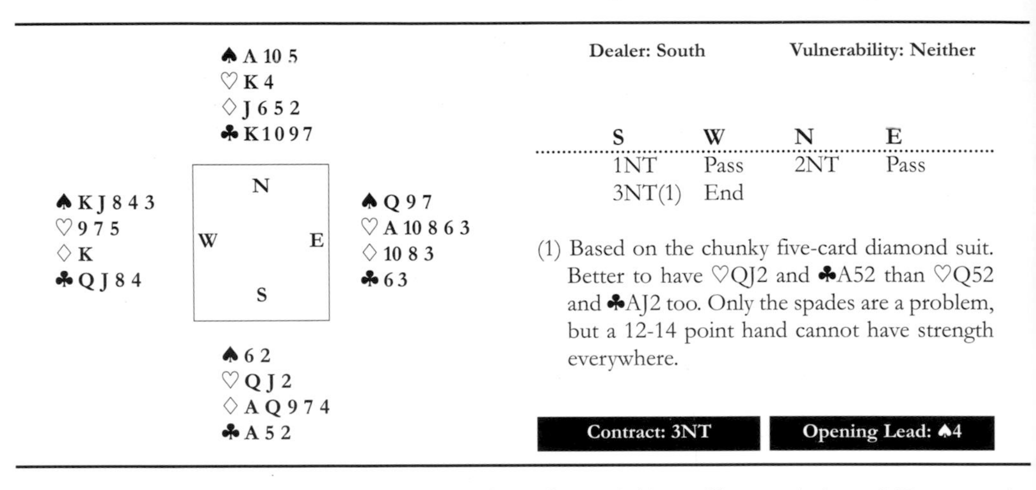

On our deal (featuring Hand (b) as North) West found the threatening spade lead, declarer playing low from dummy and East correctly inserting the nine (in case declarer held the king without the jack). This won, so East followed with the queen (top of two remaining) and a third spade to dummy's ace.

The play of the spades made it fairly clear that West held two long cards so he had to be kept out of the lead. Nine tricks were nigh-on impossible without a heart, so at Trick Four declarer led dummy's king of hearts. As hoped, East won the ace (ducking better?) and led a second heart.

Winning the heart in hand, declarer now needed just four diamond tricks and to this end he maximised his chances of avoiding West winning a trick. He cashed the ace of diamonds (key play) and his extra chance came in - West's singleton king was dropped. He could now cash four more rounds plus his top club and third top heart. In his quest to make nine tricks, he had made ten. Game made plus one.

Deal 24

Question: What do the following three hands have in common?

(a)	(b)	(c)
♠ A 2	♠ 3	♠ Q 9 8 2
♡ K 7	♡ Q 9 6 2	♡ A J 4
◇ Q 9 8 6 4 3 2	◇ A J 7 4	◇ J 4 2
♣ J 6	♣ K J 8 3	♣ K J 7

Answer: They each have three same-length suits.

The 7222, 4441 and 4333 shapes all have a habit of disappointing in the play. So much better to have - say - a 7321 than a 7222 shape. So much better to have - say - a 5431 shape than a 4441. So much better to have - say - a 4432 shape than a 4333.

People say of the 4333, 'Perfect notrump shape'. Nonsense! With just one four-card suit, even notrumps will be tough going; it's just that 4333 is little use elsewhere.

We'll consider the tricky 4441 next page, but now let us now see the 7222 disappoint:

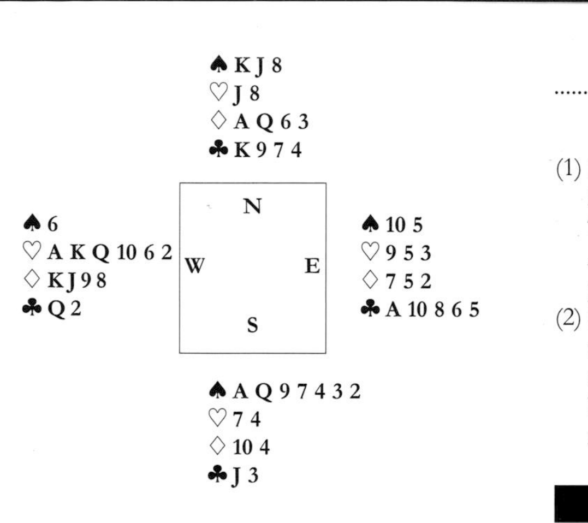

Dealer: South **Vulnerability: Both**

S	W	N	E
3♠(1)	4♡	4♠(2)	End

(1) Normal enough, perhaps, but that 7222 shape is a warning. If South was playing the Weak Two opener, he'd be well advised to use that. A 7222 shape has about the same offensive potential as, say, a 6331.

(2) Known ten-card fit make this pretty automatic. Remember the words of US teacher-expert Larry Cohen: 'When in doubt, bid 4♠ over 4♡'. It's the bid the opponents normally do not want to hear.

Contract: 4♠ **Opening Lead: ♥A**

West cashed two top hearts vs 4♠, switching to the jack of diamonds (good card - declarer can run a low diamond switch around to his ten). Declarer successfully finessed dummy's queen, drew trumps, then (his only hope) led a club to the king. East won the ace and led a second club over to West's queen. Down one.

You may say 'unlucky', but declarer would only have succeeded if both minor-suit finesses had succeeded. Better to defend 4♡ (doubled?) which goes down two on a spade lead to South's ace and a switch to the ten of diamonds leading to a third-round ruff (with a club to come). Down two.

North would not have bid 4♠ over 4♡ in spite of Larry Cohen) if South had opened a Weak Two. Perhaps worth considering (if you play Weak Twos - recommended) is to open at the Two-level with a 7222 shape, as opposed to at the Three-level. I have a shrewd suspicion that your side will judge the bidding better as a result.

Deal 25

I am sure you have experienced the problems of the 4441 shape. They are tricky to bid and often disappoint in the play.

My advice with a 12-point 4441 shape is not to open the bidding. Open and you are very likely to have to tell a lie with your rebid - remember that bidding two suits normally shows a 5-4 shape. Pass and perhaps the opponents will open your singleton suit in which case you can bid your three-suiter in one fell swoop by making a take-out double.

You should be keener to defend than declare with a 4441 shape - after all none of the opposing suits are going to split 2-2 / 3-2 / 3-3. The only danger of defending is that you are likely to have discarding problems - for it is normally unwise to throw from four-card suits. You'll have to do precisely that - unless you beat a hasty exit from the table.

North
♠ 4
♡ K 6 3 2
♢ A K J 7
♣ J 4 3 2

West
♠ A K J 9 7
♡ 10 8 4
♢ 5
♣ A K 8 5

East
♠ Q 3
♡ Q 9 7
♢ 10 9 6
♣ Q 10 9 7 6

South
♠ 10 8 6 5 2
♡ A J 5
♢ Q 8 4 3 2
♣ -

Dealer: North **Vulnerability: Neither**

S	W	N	E
		Pass(1)	Pass
Pass	1♠	Dbl(2)	Pass(3)
4♢(4)	Pass	5♢(5)	End

(1) Wisely passing the 12-point 4441 shape, anticipating rebid problems.
(2) North's dream auction materialises, enabling him to show his hand in one bid (via a take-out double), which (left to his own devices) he'd be unable to do in two bids.
(3) The obligation to dredge up a response has gone - his partner now has another bid.
(4) Excellent evaluation facing a likely singleton spade and four-card diamond support. It is the combination of no wasted values in spades plus the ninth trump that South values so highly - two important issues we will be focussing on later in our series.
(5) Because of his good trumps. If partner had bid, say, 4♣ instead, he'd have passed.

Contract: 5♦ **Opening Lead: ♠A**

If - on our deal - North opens the normally recommended 1♡ (with 1♠4♡4♢4♣), you can see North-South's auction progressing 1♡ - 1♠ - 2♣(?) - 2♡ - end, the diamond fit never mentioned.

Not that the resulting 5♢ - with just 19 high-card points - was a cinch. West led the ace of spades and switched to his trump (best). Winning in dummy, declarer ruffed a club and led a second trump to dummy, West discarding a heart). He ruffed a second club, ruffed a second spade (low) and led a heart to the jack, the finesse successful.

Declarer ruffed a third spade with dummy's last (high) trump, crossed to his ace of hearts, drew East's last trump with his queen, led over to dummy's king of hearts, and scored his 11th trick with dummy's long heart.

Fortune favours the brave!

Deal 26

Shape really is the key to Bridge. In case you are curious, here are the top 10 shapes of hands (and of suits around the table) in frequency order: 4432, 5332, 5431, 5422, 4333, 6322, 6421, 6331, 5521, 4441. You will pick up more than seven 4432s for every 4441 (yes, really).

My favourite of all the common hand patterns is the 5431 - having four suits all of different lengths is very powerful. Three possible trump suits, ruffing power, length potential. The 5431 has it all.

Dealer: North **Vulnerability: Neither**

S	W	N	E
		1♢	Pass
1♡	Pass	1♠(1)	Pass
1NT(2)	Pass	2♡(3)	Pass
4♡(4)	End		

North: ♠ A K 5 3, ♡ K 6 2, ♢ A 8 7 5 2, ♣ 4

West: ♠ J 9 4, ♡ 8 7, ♢ 10 9 6 3, ♣ A Q 10 7

East: ♠ Q 10 7 2, ♡ Q 9 4, ♢ K J, ♣ K 9 5 3

South: ♠ 8 6, ♡ A J 10 5 3, ♢ Q 4, ♣ J 8 6 2

(1) Showing the 5♢- 4♠ shape.
(2) 7-10 with no fit and clubs stopped(ish).
(3) Showing the 4♠-3♡-5♢-1♣ shape and implying some extra values (no assurance of a fit so might pass 1NT with a rank minimum 4♠-3♡-5♢-1♣).
(4) Lovely development opposite. South's hearts - including the precious ♡J10 - are upgraded in significance; whilst his mediocre clubs have ceased to become a liability - indeed the lack of wasted values facing partner's known singleton are now a positive asset.

Contract: 4♥ **Opening Lead: ♥8**

On our featured deal, it was North's third suit that proved to be the fit. West led a trump vs the resulting 4♡, knowing dummy had a singleton club. The lead ran to South's ten, at Trick Two declarer leading a club to void dummy.

The defence won the club and led another trump, declarer winning with dummy's king and leading a low diamond towards his queen (as he needed to). East hopped in with the king and led his third trump, preventing even one club ruff.

Declarer won the third trump in hand, cashed the queen of diamonds, crossed to the king of spades and cashed the ace of diamonds hoping for an even split. The diamonds were not 3-3 (East discarding on the ace). However declarer trumped a fourth diamond, crossed to the ace of spades and discarded a losing club on the promoted fifth diamond.

Declarer had to concede two clubs later on, but two spades, five trumps, the ace of diamonds, the queen of diamonds and (crucially) the long diamond meant 10 tricks and game made.

Deal 27

Contrast: (i) *KQ* facing *65432* with
(ii) *32* facing *KQ654*.

Regardless of the location of the missing ace, only one of KQ will score in Layout (i). Plus your chances of setting up the suit are hampered by the blockage and likely entry problem.

Layout (ii) is altogether much more promising - twice leading towards the king and queen; catch a 3-3 split with the ace sitting in front of (i.e. playing before) those picture cards and the suit will provide four tricks.

Similarly, contrast: (i) *AK* facing *J5432* with
(ii) *32* facing *AKJ54*

You'd much rather tackle (ii) - you have a finesse of the jack and no communication problems.

The key is having the honours in the longer length. Contrast these hands:

(a)		(b)	
♠	KQ	♠	KQ932
♡	9852	♡	52
◇	QJ	◇	QJ98
♣	A9742	♣	A4

Same high-card points and shape, yet Hand (b) rates to be way more powerful.

North
♠ K J 6 3
♡ A 9 7 4 2
◇ 9 5
♣ Q 10

West
♠ Q 7 4
♡ J 10 8
◇ A K 8 3
♣ J 8 5

East
♠ A 10
♡ 6 5 3
◇ 10 7 6 4 2
♣ K 6 3

South
♠ 9 8 5 2
♡ K Q
◇ Q J
♣ A 9 7 4 2

Dealer: South **Vulnerability: Neither**

S	W	N	E
1♣(1)	Pass	1♡	Pass
1♠(2)	Pass	3♠(3)	Pass
Pass(4)	Pass		

(1) Yuk - all those honours in the short suits. Barely an opening bid, really.
(2) Showing the 5♣-4♠ shape - nervously given his lack of pictures there.
(3) Almost a 4♠ bid - with nice picture cards facing partner's length and no wasted picture cards facing partner's shortage.
(4) Quick as a flash.

Contract: 3♠ **Opening Lead: ♦A**

On our deal South managed to scramble home in 3♠ - but it was a real struggle even opposite a suitable dummy. West led out the ace-king of diamonds (you see the value - not - of South's queen-jack) and switched to the jack of hearts.

Declarer won the queen of hearts, cashed the king, then led a trump to dummy's jack. East won the ace and led back the ten (as good as anything). Declarer won dummy's king, cashed the ace of hearts (seeing the 3-3 split) and followed with two long hearts.

It would have done West no good to ruff - with no convenient exit. However discarding only prolonged his agony, for after cashing the hearts, declarer exited with a third trump (key play). West won and switched to a low club (best - a diamond would give ruff-and-discard), but declarer knew that East would have switched to a club when in with ace of trumps if he had not held the king. He inserted dummy's ten, attracting East's king. The ace - then the promoted queen - won. Nine tricks made - phew!

Deal 28

Contrast these two hands:

(a)	(b)
♠ J 6 2	♠ J 6 2
♡ 9 7	♡ J 7 2
◇ K Q J 4 2	◇ K 7 5 4 2
♣ 8 6 3	♣ Q 6

Say the bidding goes like this:

2♣ - 2◇ - 2NT.

Partner's 2♣ shows any hand with 23+ points and, over your 2◇ negative (any hand with up to seven points, his 2NT rebid shows 23-24 balanced. The question is: should you look for slam with either (a) or (b)?

Decided? Now let us look at a possible hand for partner

♠ A K Q 2
♡ A K 3
◇ A 6
♣ A 9 7 2

6NT has 12 top tricks facing (a) - assuming diamonds are no worse than 4-2. Yet 6NT is dreadful facing (b) - indeed nine tricks may be the limit. The difference is the source of tricks - in diamonds - contained in (a). I've said it before: it's tricks not points that matter in Bridge. Although (a) and (b) both have seven points (and similar shape), (a) rates to be far stronger.

Dealer: South **Vulnerability: Neither**

S	W	N	E
1♡	Pass	2◇	Pass
3♡(1)	Pass	4♡	Pass
4NT(2)	Pass	5◇(3)	Pass
5NT(4)	Pass	7NT(5)	End

(1) Forcing to game facing a Two-over-One response.
(2) Roman Key Card Blackwood. Facing a Two-over-One response, it is reasonable for South to try for slam.
(3) One or four of 'five aces' (incl. ♡K).
(4) Showing all the key cards and ostensibly asking for kings.
(5) The masterstroke. North can deduce that South's hand, the 5NT bid indicating all the keycards, must be precisely ♡KQ(J)xxx plus the three side aces. North can count 13 tricks: six hearts, five diamonds and the two black-suit aces. Note - critically - that he chooses to play in notrumps. Those 13 tricks - available in notrumps - may not be available in hearts because of possible communication troubles should South's ace of diamonds be singleton (as here).

North: ♠ 8 5 2 ♡ A 4 ◇ K Q J 10 3 ♣ 9 7 6

West: ♠ K J 9 4 ♡ 9 8 5 ◇ 9 7 ♣ Q 10 8 4

East: ♠ Q 10 6 ♡ 10 6 ◇ 8 6 5 4 2 ♣ K 5 3

South: ♠ A 7 3 ♡ K Q J 7 3 2 ◇ A ♣ A J 2

Contract: 7NT **Opening Lead: ♥9**

On our deal North was able to count 13 tricks in the bidding - thanks to his trick source in diamonds. The ensuing 7NT did not pose a problem for South. He carefully won the (passive - but communication-cutting to the careless) heart lead in hand, unblocked the ace of diamonds, crossed to the ace of hearts, cashed ◇KQJ10 throwing black-suit losers, then crossed to a black ace to enjoy his remaining hearts and the other black ace. 13 tricks made.

Fascinatingly, 10 tricks are the limit in a heart contract - you cannot finish drawing trumps in dummy then cash diamonds.

Deal 29

There is some confusion about the value of an ace. In short, they are undervalued at four points. Don't get me wrong - I'm as nervous as the next person opening 1NT with:

♠ A 6 2
♡ 9 7
◇ A 8 4 2
♣ A 9 6 3

'Aces and spaces' and all that. However I am reminded of the (apocryphal?) story in which the late English International John Collings decided (as dealer) to make a trap pass holding ten solid spades and three small singletons. His partner passed in third chair and the hand was passed out. Collings enquired (trying to sound casual) of his partner what he held. 'Oh, just the three bare aces'!

Aces are particularly valuable when backed up by other honours: a suit of AJ102 is worth more than five points, whilst a suit of J102 may be worth nothing. Aces are also valuable when partner has a long suit. Say you open 1NT and partner, holding:

♠ J 6 2
♡ 9 7
◇ 4 2
♣ A K Q 8 5 2

makes the well-judged bid of 3NT (after all - he does have six tricks, far more than some cheesy flat 13 on which we would all bid 3NT.

Here are two possible 1NT openers you might hold:

(a)	(b)
♠ K Q 9 7	♠ A 9 7 3
♡ A 4	♡ A 4
◇ K Q 6 5	◇ A 8 6 3
♣ 10 9 7	♣ 10 9 7

Although in point-count terms (a) is maximum and (b) is minimum, it is (b) that renders 3NT an easy make, whilst the likely heart lead will see (a) fail by two tricks.

North
♠ K J
♡ 10 5
◇ A K 9 6 5 3
♣ 8 3 2

West
♠ Q 9 7 6
♡ 8 3
◇ 8 4
♣ K J 6 5 4

East
♠ 10 5 4 3
♡ A K Q J
◇ J 10 7
♣ Q 10

South
♠ A 8 2
♡ 9 7 6 4 2
◇ Q 2
♣ A 9 7

Dealer: North **Vulnerability: Neither**

S	W	N	E
		1◇	Pass(1)
1♡	Pass	2◇	Pass
3NT(2)	End		

(1) Might double for take-out.
(2) The key bid. Just 10 points facing a minimum opener, but South appreciates the value of his three high cards. The two aces are more valuable than two king-queens - being two top tricks - given that partner has long diamonds to run. Plus South loves his queen in partner's suit, bound to help those diamonds to run.

Contract: 3NT **Opening Lead: ♣5**

On our featured deal North-South made 3NT holding just 21 high-card points: it was the combination of the long diamonds and side-suit top tricks that did it. South won the club lead to East's queen with his ace (duck and East cashes four hearts). He cashed the queen of diamonds, correctly dismissed East's (clever) falsecard of the jack and led over to the ◇AK965. ♠AK brought his trick tally to nine. Game made.

Deal 30

Order these six potential opening hands. Would you pass up the opportunity with any?

(a)	(b)	(c)
♠ A 9 7 2	♠ K 8 6 5 2	♠ A Q 7 2
♡ Q 4	♡ A 9 7 2	♡ 9 4
♢ Q 2	♢ Q 2	♢ 5 2
♣ K 8 6 5 2	♣ Q 4	♣ K Q 8 6 2

(d)	(e)	(f)
♠ A 9 7 2	♠ K Q 8 6 2	♠ A Q 7 2
♡ K 8 6 5 2	♡ A Q 7 2	♡ K Q 8 6 2
♢ Q 2	♢ 5 2	♢ 5 2
♣ Q 4	♣ 9 4	♣ 9 4

There are two key factors here.

(1). Whether the honours are in the long suits (good) or the short suits (bad). Immediately you mark up (c), (e) and (f). Indeed so important is this factor that those will form your top three.

(2) Whether you have a convenient rebid. The trouble with a hand such as (f) is that, after opening 1♡, you will be awkwardly placed if partner responds (say) 2♣. To rebid 2♠ risks going overboard ('Reversers' would insist on 16 points). You'd have to rebid 2♡, although rebidding a five-card suit is something you should only do with a heavy heart. Much better to have five spades and four hearts [an easy 1♠ then 2♡ - as in (e)].

I would mark the hands (best first): (e), (c), (f), (b), (a), (d) [preferring (e) to (c) as I have both majors]. I would open (e), (c), (f) and (b) at both vulnerabilities; (a) only when non-vulnerable; and (d) not at all (yes - in spite of it satisfying the Rule of 20).

North: ♠ K ♡ A 8 6 3 ♢ A K 10 7 5 4 ♣ A 3

West: ♠ J 4 ♡ 10 7 5 2 ♢ Q 9 6 ♣ K Q 9 7

East: ♠ Q 9 6 5 3 ♡ 9 ♢ J 8 ♣ J 10 8 6 2

South: ♠ A 10 8 7 2 ♡ K Q J 4 ♢ 3 2 ♣ 5 4

Dealer: South **Vulnerability: Neither**

S	W	N	E
1♠(1)	Pass	2♢	Pass
2♡	Pass	4NT(2)	Pass
5♠(3)	Pass	7♡(4)	End

(1) Honours in long suits and an easy rebid.
(2) Roman Key Card Blackwood (hearts).
(3) Two of 'five aces' (incl. ♡K); plus ♡Q.
(4) All the keycards are held and North envisages his partner setting up his long diamonds, able to throw a second club on the ace of spades. And so it proved.

Contract: 7♥ **Opening Lead: ♣K**

Having all his honours in his long suits and an easy rebid saw this page's South stretch to open the bidding. He soon saw himself declaring a grand slam.

Declarer won the club lead with dummy's ace and led over to his ♡KQ, East following with the nine (crucially) then discarding. Postponing trumps, declarer crossed to the ace-king of diamonds (both following), cashed the blocking king of spades, then ruffed a third diamond with the jack of trumps. He cashed the ace of spades throwing dummy's club, finessed the eight of trumps, cashed the ace and followed with the three long diamonds. 13 tricks and grand slam made. Would they have even got to Six if South had passed as dealer? I doubt it.

Deal 31

Your initial evaluation of a Bridge hand (i.e. before the bidding has begun) should include a consideration of the following:

(i) High-card points, (ii) Shape, (iii) Intermediates, (iv) Honours: sequential? (v) Honours: in long suits? (vi) At least one ace? (vii) Easy rebid? As soon as the bidding begins, a whole host of other factors come into play, such as whether you like partner's suit.

Exercise: Say the bidding goes 1♡ - 2♢ - ? You must decide whether to rebid 2♡ (up to about 15 points) or jump to 3♡ (16+).

(a)		(b)	
♠	A 9 2	♠	A 9 2
♡	A K J 7 6 3	♡	A K J 7 6 3
♢	3	♢	Q 6 2
♣	Q 6 2	♣	3

There is no reason to upgrade (a); rebid 2♡. (b), however, is appreciably improved in the light of partner's 2♢ bid. The validity of this is clear when you see partner's hand (across):

♠ 10 6 2
♡ Q
♢ A K 9 5 4
♣ 8 7 5 4

Put responder's hand facing Opener (a) and you see that there's no game [3NT appears to have nine tricks but a spade lead takes out declarer's entry; he will have to overtake the queen of hearts and hope for a 3-3 split]. The bidding should go 1♡ - 2♢ - 2♡ - end.

Put responder's hand facing Opener (b), however, and it is a completely different kettle of fish. The side diamond meshing sees declarer able to make no fewer than 12 tricks on normal splits (six hearts, five diamonds and the ace of spades). Yet unless Opener (b) appreciates the improved worth of his ♢Q62, the bidding might embarrassingly stop in 2♡. I'm not suggesting the partnership will reach Six, but at least they should get to Four via 1♡ - 2♢ - 3♡ - 4♡.

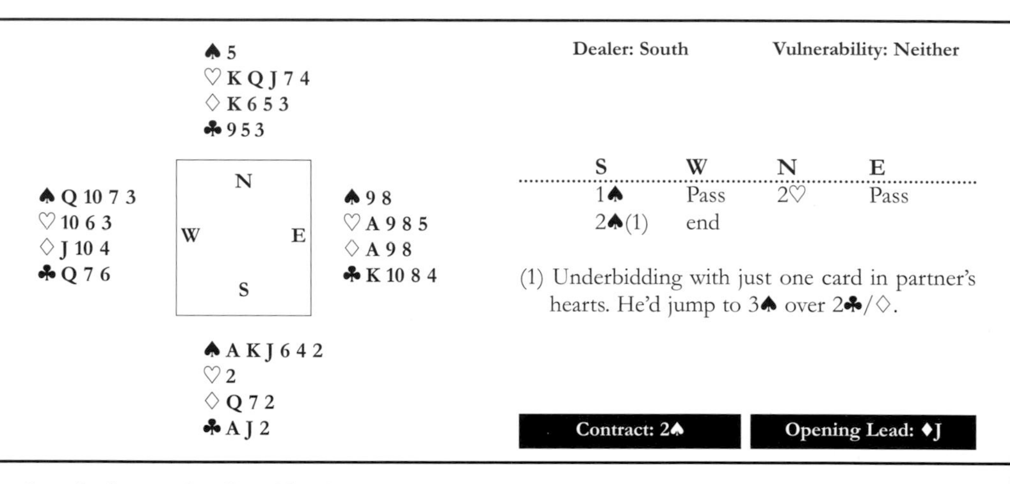

Our deal sees the flip side. South went low with 2♠ - but even that contract could not be made. Trick One went ♢J, ♢3, ♢9 (encouraging), ♢Q; Trick Two went ♡2, ♡3 (low showing an odd number), ♡K, ♡A. East switched to a surrounding-dummy's-♣9 ♣10, covered by jack and queen. Trick Four went ♣7, ♣9, ♣K, ♣A. Declarer exited with a club but West won the six and led the ten of diamonds (winning) and a third diamond to East's ace. West had to score two trumps and that meant down two.

Deal 32

We are all searching for an eight-card fit. However do not underestimate the power of the ninth trump. Whether it be for setting up a suit, extra ruffs or general control, a 5-4 fit normally plays a lot better than a 5-3 fit.

Exercise: You hold

♠ A Q 7 6 2
♡ A J 9 3
♢ 2
♣ J 10 3

and hear one of these auctions:

(i) 1♠ - 2♢ - 2♡ - 3♠ - ?
(ii) 1♠ - 3♠ - ?

Partner has shown similar strength - about 10-11 points in both auctions. But there is a fundamental difference. In (i) he has just three spades [he'd have supported immediately with four]; in (ii) he has guaranteed four spades - you have the ninth trump.

I would pass in auction (i) and raise to 4♠ in auction (ii). Let us see the two responding hands:

(i)		(ii)	
♠	K 8 4	♠	K 8 4 3
♡	5 2	♡	5 2
♢	A Q 9 6 3	♢	A Q 9 6
♣	Q 5 2	♣	Q 5 2

Yes, you might make 4♠ facing Responder (i), but you'd need 3-2 trumps and something very good to happen in the red suits. And you might go down in 4♠ facing Responder (ii) - if the opponents negotiated a club ruff, or because of a combination of 3-1 trumps and unfavourable splits in the red suits. However you'd want to be in 4♠ on (ii) and stop in 3♠ on (i). The ninth trump makes the difference.

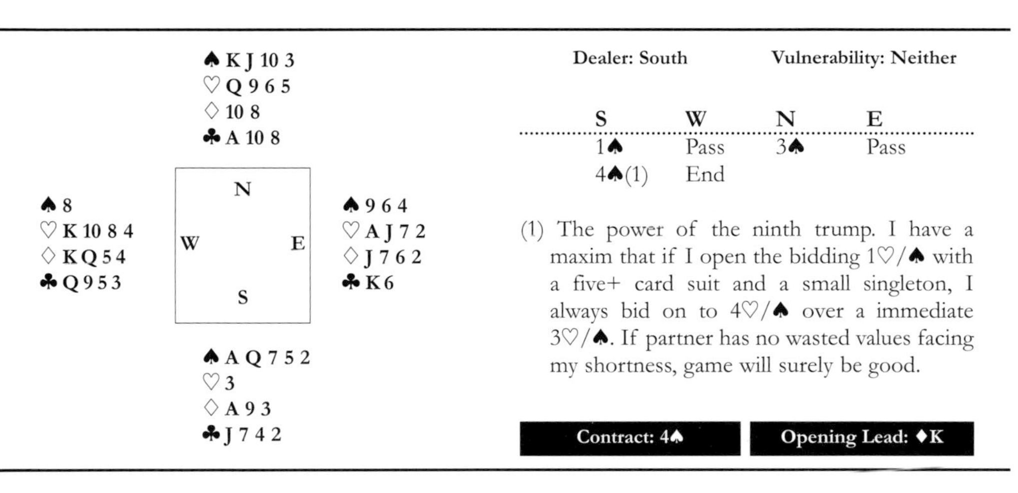

North: ♠ K J 10 3 ♡ Q 9 6 5 ♢ 10 8 ♣ A 10 8

West: ♠ 8 ♡ K 10 8 4 ♢ K Q 5 4 ♣ Q 9 5 3

East: ♠ 9 6 4 ♡ A J 7 2 ♢ J 7 6 2 ♣ K 6

South: ♠ A Q 7 5 2 ♡ 3 ♢ A 9 3 ♣ J 7 4 2

Dealer: South **Vulnerability: Neither**

S	W	N	E
1♠	Pass	3♠	Pass
4♠(1)	End		

(1) The power of the ninth trump. I have a maxim that if I open the bidding 1♡/♠ with a five+ card suit and a small singleton, I always bid on to 4♡/♠ over a immediate 3♡/♠. If partner has no wasted values facing my shortness, game will surely be good.

Contract: 4♠ **Opening Lead: ♦K**

On our featured deal, West led the king of diamonds, declarer ducking, and a second diamond to the jack and ace. At Trick Three declarer cut defensive communications by leading his heart, East winning and returning a trump.

Winning in dummy, declarer ruffed a heart then led a small club to dummy's eight (key play - finessing against the nine). East won the king and returned a second trump (West discarding). Winning again in dummy, declarer ruffed a third heart, finessed the ten of clubs, ruffed a fourth heart, ruffed his third diamond, finally drew East's third trump and cashed the ace of clubs. 10 tricks and game made on semi-unplanned Dummy Reversal lines.

Deal 33

Having a high card in partner's long suit(s) - a 'Golden Card' - is a huge asset. To fully see why, put this opener's hand:

♠ A Q 7 2
♡ 5 3 2
◇ 2
♣ A Q J 4 2

with these two responding hands:

(a)	(b)
♠ K J 6 2	♠ K J 6 2
♡ 9 7	♡ 9 7
◇ K 9 7 4 2	◇ 9 7 5 4 2
♣ 6 3	♣ K3

After the start: 1♣ - 1◇ - 1♠ - ? Hand (a) should content itself with a raise to 2♠, which opener would pass. Hand (a) facing the opener would be unlikely to yield more than nine tricks, very possibly (king of clubs offside in a 4-2 split) a struggle for eight.

Hand (b) is a different matter - thanks to the possession of the king in partner's clubs. Because of that Golden Card, Hand (b) should upgrade to a 3♠ bid [after 1♣ - 1◇ - 1♠] whereupon opener, with his pretty 5431 shape and all his honours in the long suits, would go on to 4♠. 4♠ would be a cinch (on a 3-2 trump split), losing just two hearts and a diamond.

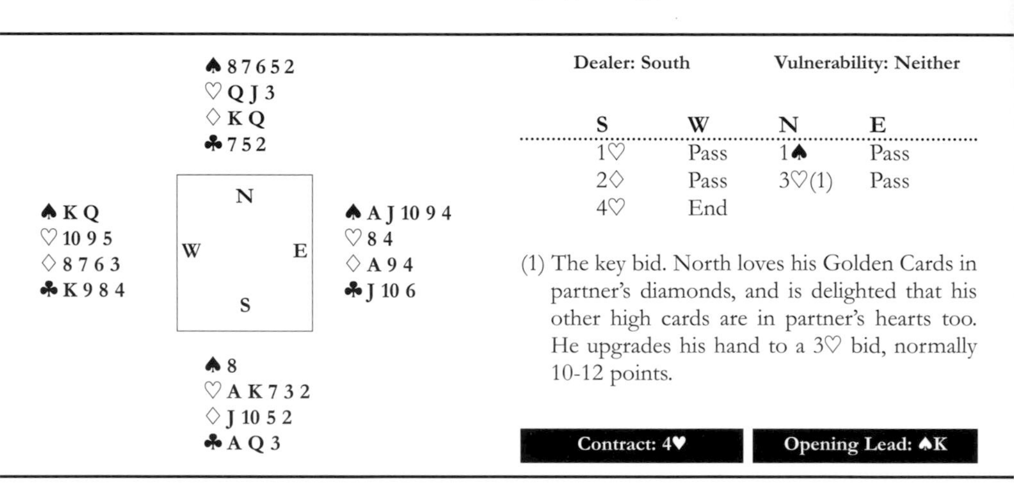

On our deal, West sensibly steered clear of the unbid clubs, East letting his king of spades lead win Trick One (overtaking with the ace and switching to a club works better). Declarer ruffed West's queen of spades continuation and led a diamond to the king and East's ace. East returned the jack of clubs, suggestive (as was West's non-lead of a club) that the king was offside.

Rising with the ace of clubs, declarer crossed to the queen of diamonds, then led queen-jack of trumps (both following). Leaving the small trump in dummy (as he had to) declarer now ruffed a spade high, West discarding a diamond, then led out jack-ten of diamonds, throwing dummy's clubs.

West had to ruff the fourth diamond - or declarer could ruff a club with dummy's small trump. But now he was endplayed to lead clubs. Whether he led low (declarer discards from dummy and the lead runs to the queen) or his actual choice of the king (ruff in dummy, ruff a spade, cash the promoted queen of clubs), it was a case of 10 tricks and game made. Not easy mind.

Deal 34

'Hard Cards' are high cards that are bound to win - essentially aces (and less so kings). 'Soft Cards' are queens (and less so jacks): cards that may win, may not.

The location of Soft Cards is in many ways more important than the Hard Cards, for the reason that aces (almost) always win tricks, whilst queens are in the balance. In evaluating the worth of your hand, look where you queens are. If they are in partner's suit(s), they are full value; if they are in opposing suits, they are potentially useless.

Exercise: You are South here:

N	W	S	E
1♢	1♠	2♡	2♠
3♡	P	?	

Would you bid on to 4♡ with either of these three hands?

(a)	(b)	(c)
♠ Q 2	♠ 6 2	♠ 6 2
♡ A K J 6 2	♡ A K J 6 2	♡ A K J 6 2
♢ 9 2	♢ 9 2	♢ Q 9
♣ 8 6 3 2	♣ Q 6 3 2	♣ 8 6 3 2

Hand (a) is a clear pass of 3♡. Partner has shown a relatively minimum opener (raising to 3♡ not 4♡) and two of your points - the soft queen of the opposing spades - are likely worth nothing.

Hand (b) is a slightly questionable raise to 4♡. Your soft queen - clubs - may or may not be useful. You'd bid 4♡ at Rubber/Teams if vulnerable (for the game bonus), perhaps not at Duplicate Pairs (where pushing for close games is generally losing tactics).

Hand (c) sees your soft card - the queen of diamonds - in partner's suit. Bid 4♡.

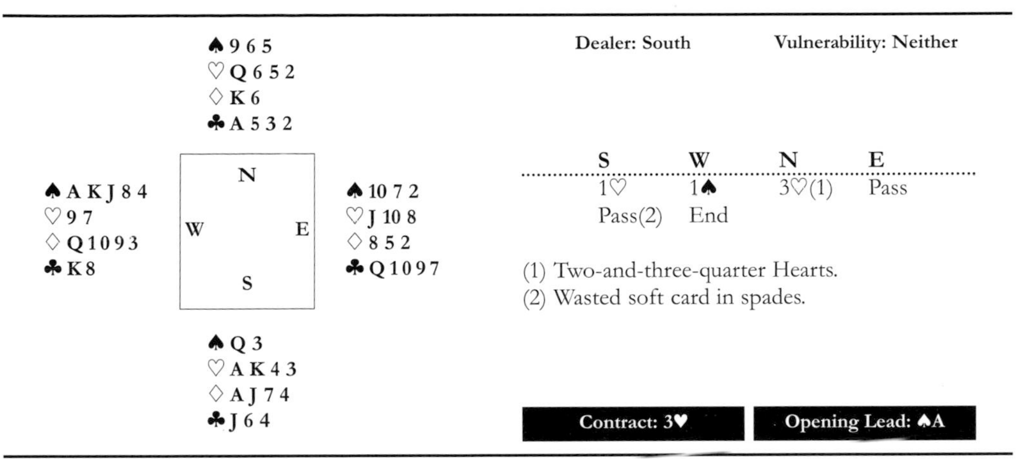

Even 3♡ was a struggle. West led out ♠AKJ, ruffed. Declarer led to the king of diamonds, back to the ace, then ruffed a diamond. He crossed to the ace of trumps then led the jack of diamonds, ruffing with dummy's queen when West played the queen (correct though it promoted East's ♡J10).

Declarer crossed to his king of trumps (both following), then led a low club, playing West for a 5♠2♡4♢2♣ shape with ♣K/Qx. West could not play the king or declarer would win the ace and lead towards his jack. However when West played a low club, declarer rose with the ace and led a second club to West's bare king.

West's forced spade lead enabled declarer to make his remaining trump en passant. For if East ruffed, declarer could throw his club; whilst if East discarded, declarer could ruff. Nine tricks made.

Deal 35

You hold as South an unsupported king. Contrast these three layouts:

(i)

West	North	East
	♠ A 2	
♠ Q 10 8 6 4		♠ J 9 7 5
	South	
	♠ K 3	

(ii)

West	North	East
	♠ 4 2	
♠ Q 10 8 6		♠ A J 9 7 5
	South	
	♠ K 3	

(iii)

West	North	East
	♠ 4 2	
♠ A Q 10 8 6		♠ J 9 7 5
	South	
	♠ K 3	

Your king is promoted in (i) as partner holds the ace. Your king can also be promoted in (ii) by leading from North towards your king. The ace being in East's hand (playing before your king), means that your king will be promoted whether or not East plays the ace. On (iii), however, the trick will go: ♠2, ♠5, ♠K, ♠A and your king cannot be promoted into a trick.

Try during the bidding to gauge the likelihood of such a king being promoted - whether partner holds the ace; or, failing that, whether the ace is more likely to be on your right (good) or your left (bad).

Exercise: The bidding has proceeded 1♠ - (2♢) - 2♠ - (3♣) - ? [Opposing bids in brackets]. What next with the following two opening hands?

	(a)	(b)
♠	A Q 8 6 4 2	A Q 8 6 4 2
♡	A J 7	A J 7
♢	3 2	K 2
♣	K 2	3 2

(a) 4♠. Well-positioned king of clubs and no wastage in diamonds.

(b) 3♠. Poorly-positioned king of diamonds plus any club honours partner has will be poorly-positioned. Bid 3♠ more to prevent the opponents from making their contract than expecting to make it.

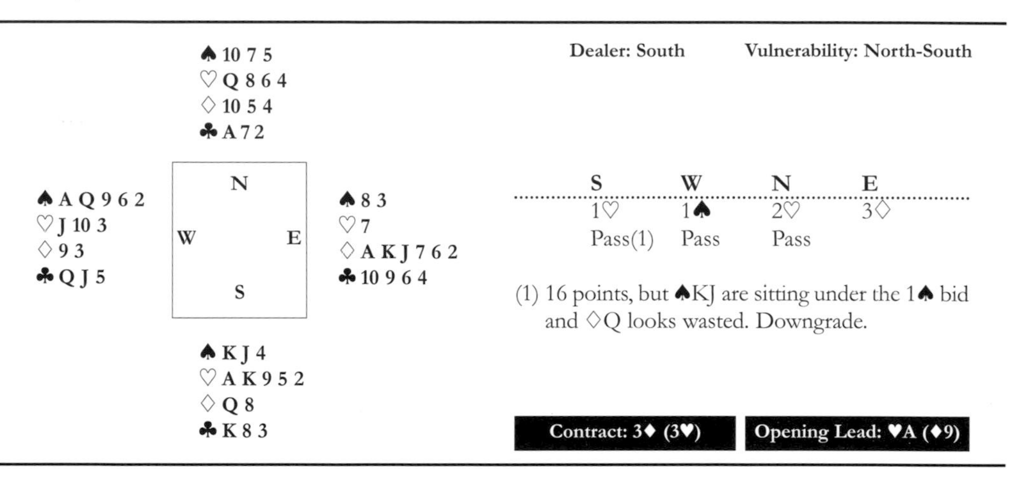

On our deal, South must resist the temptation to bid 3♡ over 3♢. 3♢ would make okay - but 3♡ would be murdered. In 3♡, East would win the nine of diamonds lead with the king and switch to the eight of spades. West would win the queen, cash the ace and lead a third spade, East ruffing then playing ace-jack of diamonds. South has to discard a club (a loser-on-loser) rather than ruff (low or high) to escape for down two.

Deal 36

When the opponents have bid and supported a suit, you can accurately evaluate your holding.

Exercise: Take this auction: 1♣ - (1♡) - 1♠ - (3♡) - ? in which the opponents have bid and supported hearts to the Three-level implying [as the overcalling side 'bidding to the level of their fit'] a nine-card fit. Rank the following opening hands, all with 13 points and support for partner's spades:

(i)	♠ A Q 3 2	♡ 4 3 2	◇ 8	♣ A Q J 4 2
(ii)	♠ A Q 3 2	♡ Q J	◇ 8 3	♣ A 9 7 4 2
(iii)	♠ A Q 3 2	♡ 3 2	◇ Q J	♣ A 9 7 4 2
(iv)	♠ A Q 3 2	♡ 3 2	◇ 8 3	♣ A Q J 9 7
(v)	♠ A Q 3 2	♡ 8 4 3 2	◇ -	♣ A Q J 4 2

Your side have four cards in hearts. The worst number of hearts for you to hold is two, for partner then also has two. Better to have three, for now partner has just one; better still to have four, for now partner has none at all. Further, having all your values outside hearts - particularly in trumps (spades) and your long clubs - is far better than having wasted points in hearts.

My order is therefore - from worst to best: (ii), (iii), (iv), (i), (v). (v) is unbelievably powerful - partner has a void heart and you have a void diamond. Give partner this seven-point hand:

♠ KJ7654
♡ -
◇ 9732
♣ K53

and you can make a grand slam - with just a combined 20 points. In effect you are playing with a 20-point pack - only 20 of the 40 points in the pack are going to win tricks - and you have all 20 of them!

North:
♠ 973
♡ A K 7 2
◇ 4
♣ A K 8 6 2

West:
♠ K 10 5 4 2
♡ J 10
◇ A 5 4 3
♣ J 5

East:
♠ A Q J 8 6
♡ 9
◇ 10 8 6 2
♣ Q 10 7

South:
♠ -
♡ Q 8 6 5 4 3
◇ K Q J 9
♣ 9 4 3

Dealer: North **Vulnerability: Neither**

S	W	N	E
		1♣	1♠
2♡	4♠(1)	6♡(2)	end

(1) Bidding to the level of the fit (there are ten spades so bid for ten tricks).

(2) North calculates that partner rates to have a void spade. He is therefore playing with a '30-point pack' in the sense that only 30 of the 40 points (i.e. outside spades) will play a role. Slam will be possible with far fewer than the normal 33 / 40.

Contract: 6♥ **Opening Lead: ♠K**

30-point packs are more common - take our featured deal in which North bids 6♡ on the basis that the 10 points in spades will take no tricks. Declarer ruffed the spade lead, drew trumps finishing in dummy, then led a diamond. He needed three discards for dummy's clubs and, when East played low, read West for the ace (it would take nerves of steel for East to duck the ace with dummy holding singleton - and be fatal on many layouts). He played the nine (key play) and was rewarded when this finesse against the ten was successful, the nine drawing West's ace. He could now discard ♣862 on ◇KQJ and claim his 22-point slam.

Deal 37

We have on preceding deals observed the importance of such factors as whether your high cards are in partner's long suits (good) or short suits (bad). Say opener holds:

♠ A K 9 5 2
♡ A 4
◇ K J 7 4
♣ 4 2

and hears partner raise his 1♠ to 2♠. Put opener's hand facing these three responding hands:

(a)	(b)	(c)
♠ Q 8 6 2	♠ Q 8 6 2	♠ Q 8 6 2
♡ Q 7	♡ 8 7 5	♡ 7 5
◇ 6 5 2	◇ Q 5 2	◇ A Q 2
♣ A 7 5 3	♣ A 7 5	♣ 7 6 5 3

All three have eight points and four-card spade support: a classic 2♠ bid. Yet opener facing (a) is a hopeless 4♠ - even 3♠ may prove too high. Facing (b), 4♠ will make and facing (c) 11 tricks are a cinch on a 2-2 / 3-1 trump split [trumps drawn then dummy's heart going on declarer's fourth diamond and the heart ruffed]. The critical factor is responder's diamond holding. Enter the *Trial Bid*, a key tool in Hand Evaluation.

A Trial Bid, essentially a natural bid, is the first bid after a suit has been bid and supported. It shows a longish (three+ cards, usually four+) weakish (normally missing two of the four top cards) suit. It asks for help in the suit - a source of losers if you like.

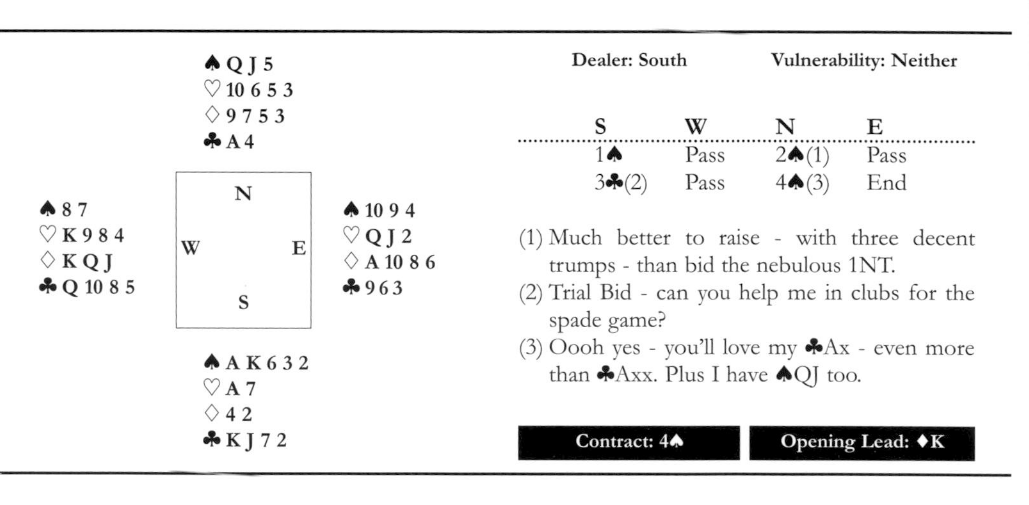

On our deal, the side-suit meshing in clubs came to light through South's 3♣ Trial Bid. The defence led three rounds of diamonds, declarer ruffing and correctly starting on clubs (draw trumps and he'll be left with the problem of the third and fourth clubs).

A club to the ace - a club to the king (no finesse) was followed by a third club ruffed low. Declarer crossed to the ace of hearts, ruffed a fourth club (with the jack), cashed the queen of trumps and faced the challenge of returning to hand to draw the three remaining trumps without being overruffed.

Declarer found the solution. He led dummy's fourth diamond and, when East covered it, discarded his remaining heart (key play). He could now ruff East's heart return with a low trump and score the last two tricks with his ace-king of trumps. 10 tricks and game made.

Deal 38

When the last bid was suit agreement, the first bid in a new suit at the lowest level should be a Trial Bid, essentially a natural bid asking for help in the bid suit. You will have a longish (three+ cards, usually four+), weakish (missing two of the top four cards) suit.

Exercise: You bid 1♡ and partner raises to 2♡. What now with:

(a)	(b)	(c)
♠ A 2	♠ A J 9	♠ 2
♡ A Q 7 5 2	♡ A K 8 2	♡ A K 9 4 2
◇ Q 2	◇ Q 9 7 3	◇ J 4 2
♣ K J 6 4	♣ K J	♣ A K J 7

(a) Bid 3♣ - showing a source of losers in clubs. Partner will normally bid 3♡ or 4♡ depending largely on his clubs.

(b) 2NT. A Trial Bid guarantees an eight-card fit. Here partner may have raised with just three hearts so you must suggest no trumps.

(c) 3◇. Ask for help in the weak diamonds, rather than the clubs that need little assistance.

Let's move across the table. If partner makes a Trial Bid, you must look first and foremost at your holding in the Trial Bid suit. One approach is to use our friend the LTC. If you have three LTs in the Trial Bid suit, sign off (bidding the trump suit at the lowest level). With one LT (or zero) accept the invite by jumping to game. With two LTs, look at your trumps, also at whether you are minimum or maximum for your earlier bid.

Exercise: Partner opens 1♡, you raise to 2♡ and partner now bids 3♣. What next with these (across):

(d)	(e)	(f)
♠ 7 5 4	♠ K Q J	♠ K 7 3
♡ K 8 6 4	♡ J 8 6 4	♡ K J 8 6
◇ 7 5 4 3	◇ J 9 7	◇ 9 4 2
♣ A 3	♣ 7 5 3	♣ Q 8 2

(d) 4♡. Great clubs - one LT - and goodish trumps. Accept.

(e) 3♡. The dreaded three small cards in the Trial Bid. Sign off.

(f) 4♡. Medium clubs - two LTs - but the trumps are good and you have a maximum point-count.

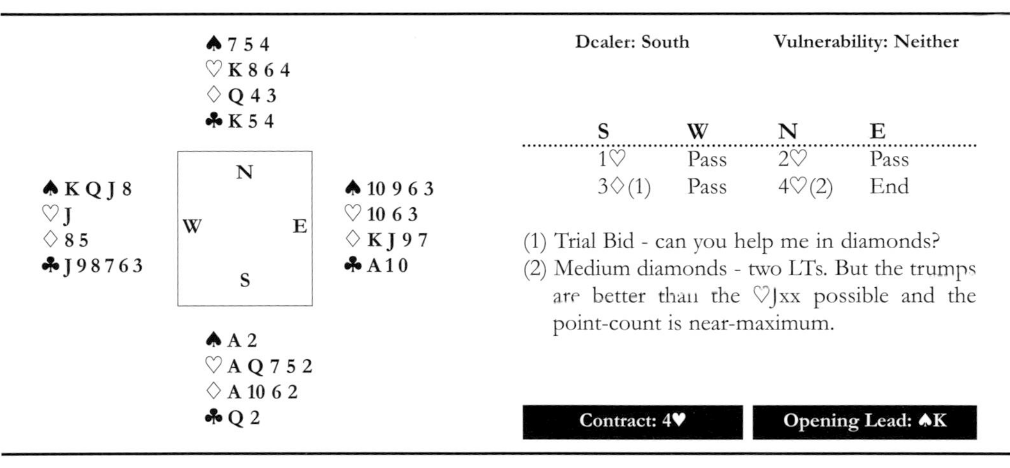

On our deal, declarer ducked ♠K, won ♠Q with ♠A, cashed ♡AQ, then led to ◇Q (hoping West held ◇K). No - East won ◇K and led ♠10.

Declarer ruffed, crossed to ♡K, then led to ◇10. This finesse successful, he cashed ◇A, ruffed ◇6 and forced out ♣A. 10 tricks and game made.

Deal 39

The first bid after suit agreement is a Trial Bid, showing a long, weak suit and asking for help in the bid suit. E.g. 1♠ - 2♠ - 3♣.

Reacting to the Trial Bid - count Losing Tricks (LTs) in the suit

Three LTs: Sign off.

Two LTs: Look at trumps and whether your point-count is good.

One LT: Accept.

Take a slightly different auction, with the responder being the Trial Bidder - same principle though: 1♡ - 1♠ - 2♠ - 3♢.

Responder could have:

(a)	or	(b)
♠ A Q 7 3 2		♠ A 10 7 3 2
♡ Q 6		♡ 6 2
♢ J 10 4 2		♢ J 7 4
♣ 9 3		♣ A 9 8

You may be a tad surprised as to how weak these hands are (to try for game). Reflect on partner's bidding. He has opened 1♡ and raised 1♠ to 2♠. Yet he cannot have a 12-14 balanced hand (no 1NT opener) so either he has extra points (15 - too strong for 1NT) or he has extra shape (i.e. unbalanced).

Opener could have:

(i)	(ii)	(iii)	(iv)
♠K J 6 4	♠K 9 6 4	♠K J 9 5	♠Q 9 6 4
♡A J 7 2	♡A K 3 2	♡A J 8 4 3	♡K J 5 4 3
♢9 3 2	♢A 3	♢3	♢Q 8
♣A Q	♣J 10 8	♣K 7 2	♣K J

Decide on opener's bid after 1♡ - 1♠ - 2♠ - 3♢ - ?

(i). 3♠. Sign off - bad diamonds.
(ii). 4♠. One LT in diamonds.
(iii). 4♠. Singleton diamond.
(iv). 3♠. Two LTs in diamonds, but aceless with mediocre trumps.

On all eight scenarios [(a) & (b) facing (i) - (iv)] good 4♠ games are bid and bad ones avoided.

Our deal sees Responder (b) facing Opener (iii) make 4♠.

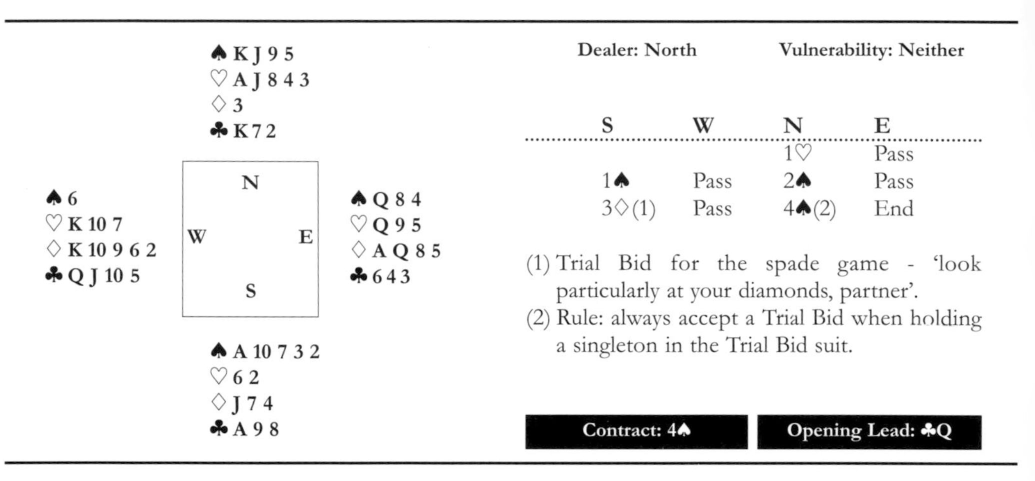

Declarer won ♣Q with ♣A and immediately led ♡2 to ♡J (correctly starting the side-suit before drawing trumps). East won ♡Q and returned ♣6 to ♣9, ♣10 and ♣K. Declarer cashed ♡A and ruffed ♡3 with ♠10. Pleased to see the 3-3 heart split, he turned to trumps, cashing ♠A and leading to ♠K. He was less fortunate here - East having ♠Q winner. However declarer now led the good ♡8 and (East ruffing with that ♠Q) shed his ♣8. He could ruff East's ♣4 in hand and merely concede a diamond. 10 tricks and game made.

Deal 40

The first bid after major-suit agreement should be a Trial Bid. In the auction 1♡ - 2♡ - 3♣, the 3♣ bid is a Trial Bid for game, asking partner to bid 3♡ or 4♡ depending (largely) on whether he has help for clubs.

Now take an auction such as 1♠ - 3♠ - 4♢. One thing is clear - the 4♢ bid must be a try for a spade slam. With interest only in game, opener would bid 4♠. Many play 4♢ as the cheapest ace-showing cue bid; but this is surely not the best use for the bid. Far better, in the quest to see whether the hands mesh well, is to play 4♢ as a Trial Bid. 'Partner, can you help me in diamonds for the spade *slam*?'

Example hands for 1♠ - 3♠ - 4♢:

(a)	(b)
♠ KQ1062	♠ AK10852
♡ A2	♡ K3
♢ KJ642	♢ QJ32
♣ A	♣ A

Note that it is partner's diamond holding that will be crucial to whether 6♠ makes or not.

Exercise: What should these 3♠ responses do after the 4♢ Trial bid?

(i)	(ii)	(ii)
♠ AJ62	♠ AJ73	♠ Q952
♡ Q7	♡ 1086	♡ A86
♢ 953	♢ A5	♢ K94
♣ KJ53	♣ J742	♣ J87

(i). Sign off in 4♠. You have the 'death holding' in diamonds - three small cards.

(ii). 6♠. Or 4NT (ace-asking). Or an ace-showing cue-bid of 5♢. Not 4♠. Put (ii) facing Opener (a) and you see that 6♠ is great.

(iii). 4♡ - an ace-showing cue-bid, showing some slam interest, (therefore inferentially help in diamonds) is the best bid. Less scientifically 5♠. Or 4NT. Even 6♠. But not 4♠. Put (iii) facing Opener (c) and you see that 6♠ is fabulous - and facing a 4♡ ace-showing cue-bid Opener would know to bid it.

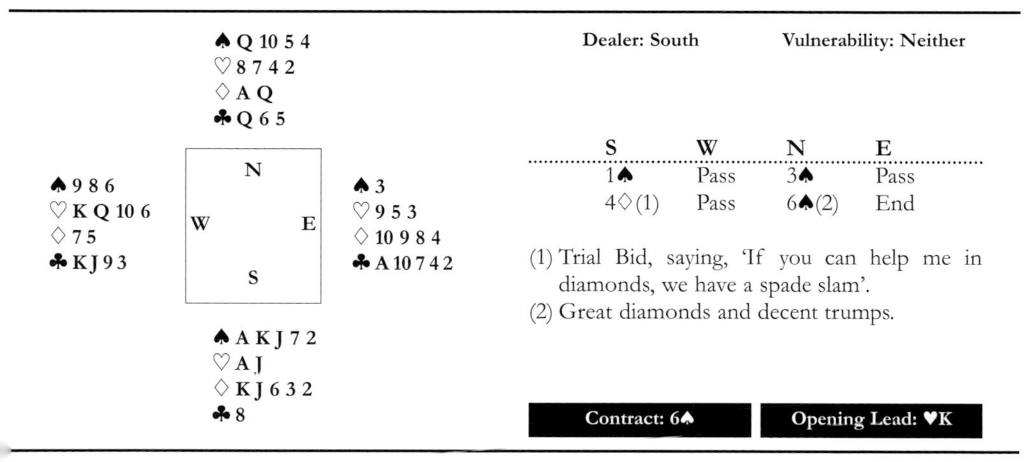

On our deal, the excellent diamond meshing, only known about through the Trial Bid, makes 6♠ look easy: three of dummy's cards in either clubs or hearts disappearing on ♢KJ6. True - but be careful.

Win ♡A, cash two top trumps (East discarding - a club), but leave the last trump out. First, crucially, unblock ♢AQ, then cross to the third trump in hand. Now play ♢KJ6 discarding (say) ♡874 (or ♣Q65) and ruff ♡J with dummy's trump. 12 tricks and slam made.

Deal 41

We have been focussing on the Trial Bid, that tool to assist in the gauging of how the side-suits mesh. Another vital tool in such assessments is the Splinter Bid - a must-play slam convention.

Contrast these three layouts:

	West (Opener)		East
(A)	♠ AK9752		♠ QJ43
	♡ 2	facing	♡ 3
	◇ KQJ		◇ A 3 2
	♣ 5 4 3		♣ A 9 8 7 6
(B)	♠ AK9752		♠ QJ43
	♡ 2	facing	♡ A 4 3
	◇ KQJ		◇ 3
	♣ 5 4 3		♣ A 9 8 7 6
(C)	♠ AK9752		♠ QJ43
	♡ 2	facing	♡ A 4 3
	◇ KQJ		◇ A 9 8 7 6
	♣ 5 4 2		♣ 3

In both (A) and (B), 4♠ is the limit, with a heart and two clubs to lose in (A) and a diamond and two clubs in (B). In (C), however, by jigging East's side-suits around (but adding no high-cards), 6♠ is easy.

The key is the location of East's singleton. Where it is facing West's singleton [as in (A)], it adds nothing; where it is facing West's KQJ [as in (B)], it similarly adds nothing. In either case West was bound to lose at most one trick in the suit regardless of East's holding. In (C), however, West's three losing clubs condense to one loser because East has a singleton. The low point-count slam makes.

The Splinter Bid shows partner the singleton. It is a double jump in a new suit that shows a singleton (or void) in the bid suit and agrees partner's suit, with game+ values.

The bidding in (A) would be 1♠ - 4♡ - 4♠. In (B): 1♠ - 4◇ - 4♠. In (C), however, it would be 1♠ - 4♣ - 4NT - 5♡* - 6♠.

** 5♠ if playing Roman Key Card Blackwood*

North: ♠ A Q 8 5 2 / ♡ A 6 5 4 / ◇ 8 / ♣ J 9 4

West: ♠ 10 4 / ♡ 9 8 7 / ◇ K J 5 / ♣ Q 8 6 5 2

East: ♠ K J 9 7 6 / ♡ 2 / ◇ Q 10 7 6 / ♣ K 10 7

South: ♠ 3 / ♡ K Q J 10 3 / ◇ A 9 4 3 2 / ♣ A 3

Dealer: South **Vulnerability: Neither**

S	W	N	E
1♡	Pass	4◇(1)	Pass
4NT(2)	Pass	5♡(2)	Pass
5NT(3)	Pass	6♣(3)	Pass
6♡	end		

(1) Splinter bid - singleton (void) diamond in a raise to (at least) 4♡.
(2) Fabulous news - length but no wasted picture cards in partner's splinter suit is perfect. South asks for aces - answer: two.
(3) How many kings? Answer: none.

Contract: 6♥ **Opening Lead: ♥7**

On our deal, declarer won West's passive ♡7 lead with ♡10 and played ◇A - ruff ◇2. He crossed to ♣A and ruffed ◇3 (low - pleased to see both opponents follow to reveal the 4-3 split). He cashed ♠A, ruffed ♠2 (with ♡3), ruffed ◇4 (with ♡A), ruffed ♠5 (with ♡J) cashed ♡KQ drawing West's ♡98 and tabled ◇9, a length winner. He merely gave up ♣3 at the end - 12 tricks and slam made.

Deal 42

Contrast:

(A)	(B)
North	**North**
♠ AQ1073	♠ AQ1073
♡ 432	♡ 432
◊ 6	◊ 6
♣ KJ32	♣ KJ32
South	**South**
♠ KJ986	♠ KJ986
♡ 765	♡ AJ
◊ KQ	◊ 432
♣ AQ4	♣ AQ4

In (A) N-S cannot even make 4♠; in (B) they make 6♠ - yet the two Norths are identical and the two Souths pretty similar. The key difference is South's diamond holding facing partner's singleton.

(A)'s diamond holding is highly unsuitable: short with five wasted points. Make ◊KQ into ♡KQ and 11 tricks would be easy. (B) has no wasted values in diamonds and more length (two ruffing tricks).

These differences can be diagnosed via the Splinter Bid. North bids 4◊ to South's 1♠ opener - a double jump in a new suit showing a singleton (void) in the bid suit and a game+ raise in spades (North has seven Losing Tricks). In (A) South would hurriedly sign off in 4♠; in (B) he would advance towards slam.

Exercise: Evaluate the following holdings facing partner's Splinter Bid. Rate them on a scale of 0 - 10.

(i) *KQ*	(ii) *32*	(iii) *432*
(iv) *KJ4*	(v) *A432*	(vi) *65432*

(i) 0/10. Short with wasted picture cards. Yuk!
(ii) 5/10. Being short is bad; having no wasted high-cards is good.
(iii) 7/10. The more cards (to be trumped) the better; the fewer potential losers you'll have outside.
(iv) 2/10. Four wasted points.
(v) 9/10. No losers and length. Ideally four small cards and the ace outside (to bolster other honours) - that's why it's not 10/10.
(vi) 10/10. Length and no wasted honours: perfect. With all strength outside, the sky is the limit.

North: ♠ AJ86 ♡ KQ982 ◊ 3 ♣ J93

West: ♠ Q109 ♡ 104 ◊ Q10975 ♣ AK7

East: ♠ - ♡ J7653 ◊ KJ ♣ Q108652

South: ♠ K75432 ♡ A ◊ A8642 ♣ 4

Dealer: South **Vulnerability: Neither**

S	W	N	E
1♠	Pass	4◊(1)	Pass
4NT(2)	Pass	5◊(2)	Pass
6♠	End		

(1) Splinter bid - short diamonds and a game+ raise in spades.
(2) Length and no wasted picture cards - fabulous news so South asks for aces (one).

Contract: 6♠ **Opening Lead: ♣A**

On our deal, West leads out ♣AK. South ruffs, cashes ♠K (retaining ♠AJ in case East discards - as here). He leads ♠3 to ♠J, back to ♡A (unblocking), over to ♠A (felling ♠Q), cashes ♡KQ (noting West's ♡10), then leads ♡9 through East's ♡J7. East (say) covers with ♡J, so South ruffs, cashes ◊A, ruffs ◊4 and cashes ♡8. 12 tricks and slam made

Deal 43

For the final page we review the key elements to accurate Hand Evaluation.

Initial Assessment:

Point-count - useful particularly in notrumps but must not be the sole method...a la 'Points Schmoints'.

Shape - upgrade hands with long suits and short suits, also ones with unequal lengths. Thumbs up to 5431, thumbs down to 4333.

Intermediates - tens (and nines) must not be ignored, especially in notrumps or when you've the jack.

Sequences - upgrade KQs, QJs, downgrade 'gappy' AJs and KJs.

Honours - upgrade them in long suits, downgrade them in short.

Reassessment during the Bidding:

Upgrade if you have...

Honours in partner's bid suits.
Honours in right-hand opponent's bid suits.
Right number of cards in opposing bid and supported suits: shortage or length so you can deduce partner is short *(see deal)*.
Trump length - the ninth trump is very powerful.

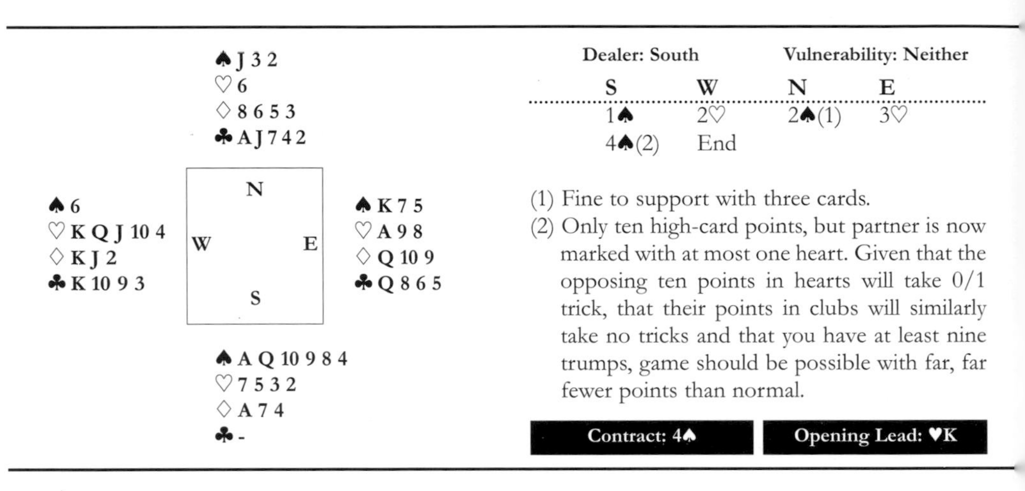

Dealer: South　　Vulnerability: Neither

S	W	N	E
1♠	2♡	2♠(1)	3♡
4♠(2)	End		

(1) Fine to support with three cards.
(2) Only ten high-card points, but partner is now marked with at most one heart. Given that the opposing ten points in hearts will take 0/1 trick, that their points in clubs will similarly take no tricks and that you have at least nine trumps, game should be possible with far, far fewer points than normal.

Contract: 4♠　　**Opening Lead: ♥K**

Our deal sees North-South attempt game with just 16 high-card points. West led the king of hearts and switched to his singleton trump to cut down ruffs in dummy (best). Declarer tried dummy's jack, in the hope of tempting East to cover with his king. East played low, however.

The problem was that declarer could not both ruff two hearts in dummy and keep a trump with which to pick up East's guarded king. However watch...

Cash dummy's ace of clubs discarding (say) heart and ruff a club. Ruff a heart, ruff a clu ruff a heart, ruff a club and play ace of diamond then exit with a diamond. Let the defence wi and cash another diamond, for your last tw cards are ♠AQ and East's are ♠K7. Regardles of which opponent is on lead, you can beat East seven of trumps with the queen and beat his kin with the ace. 10 tricks and game made.

Final thought on Hand Evaluation: *Thin Tricks not Points.*